THE BOOK
OF RAIN

By

Anthony Weirich

Dedication

To my wife who took many chances on me when you didn't have to.

This would not be possible without you.

Acknowledgments

Over the years and decades, I have crossed paths with many people that I would consider my friends and family. I asked them to look at what I wrote and tell me if the stories were going in the right direction and if they kept them engaged.

The responses were overall positive, to say the least, but I felt that needed a few extra pushes to allow me to finish the story the way it should be finished.

The journeys and the stories like these insides will be ever-changing, and at any moment it may be necessary to tell another tale, if there is time for me to tell it.

I would like to thank the ones who read my tales and I hope the story was strong enough for them to recommend this to someone else.

About the Author

Anthony Weirich would be considered a Jack-of-all-Trades in profession, in travel, in life, and in mind.

He is a Halloween baby who was born in Wisconsin. He spent the 1970's being raised in Northern Indiana by his mother Judy, the first of his stepfathers, along with his sister Amy, brother Nick, and stepsiblings, Charlie and Dwayne.

He finished his time in school, back in Southern Wisconsin trying to find a place to fit in. Stories, poems, and dreams were his escape.

He spent some time in Seattle in the 1990's trying to find himself.

That's where he found Rain and Emily with a story to tell.

Anthony returned to Wisconsin to reset himself and to work in the communities he lived.

That was where he found Matt. He had a story to tell.

In the 2000's he chose his new path by living in Dallas.

He grew up. Tried to do different opportunities that were not presented to him living in Wisconsin.

That is when he found Pamela and Rachel. They had a story that needed to be told.

He worked retail, sales and thanks to a friend that changed his life, a management and customer service job that he was not fired or released from.

In 2012, at a high school reunion in Southern Wisconsin, he crossed paths and hearts with his now and forever wife.

After an editor questioned the length of his story, he thought he completed, he sat down and gave it some thought.

That was when he found Naomi. She had a story to be told.

Anthony currently works a Medicare Healthcare Advisor. His wife is a College Professor in the field of Early Childcare. They foster for the Humane Society, and they also try to give assistance their community whenever the need arises.

They live currently in Southern Wisconsin, with four adult cats.

Table of Contents

Chapter One - Emily

Even before the first light of day shone, she could see children playing in an expansive field of trees, shrubs, and tall grass. The children wore everything from dresses, jeans, shorts, blouses, and T-shirts. They ran around in tennis shoes, dress shoes, socks, sandals, and bare feet in frenzied delight. They played various games of tag, hide-and-seek, and red light/green light, filling the air with laughter. When they had nearly exhausted themselves, they would stop to catch their breath, then start up again, running toward and away from one another.

She soared above them wanting to join but decided to leave them be. In the pale morning light, she could see the flowing colors of their hair and clothes circling around each other in graceful patterns. It reminded her of the art-painting books she had collected.

A small breeze pushed her away from the children and escorted her to a place above a winding creek. The tall, lush willow trees guarded both sides of the creek's banks. Their long, hanging strands of leaf-heavy branches touched the water with their tips, brushing its surface. The sound of water clapping rose as the water lapped against the muddy banks. She could smell the aroma of the trees and taste the water's mist in the air.

She viewed a small, flat wooden raft floating aimlessly on the stream, semi-concealed by the hanging willows. "He could be there," she said, "lying on his back, one bare foot in the water, holding a fishing stick made from one of those branches, looking skyward, and chewing on a blade of grass."

She willed herself toward a large, familiar oak tree. It was tall and wide, with roots dug deeply into the earth. The mighty tree watched over her backyard, protecting it from the ravages of the summer sun. It also housed the small birds and animals that ran throughout the yard.

She maneuvered toward the green leaves that grew during the times of early spring. Within the foliage, closer to the trunk, she found the nest holding the newborn robins. She had never been able to get this close before and simply wanted to see them.

Her eyes adjusted to the dark shadows and found five babies. Their beaks lifted high in a chaotic choir call for their mother and the food she regularly provided. They had no feathers; their skin was pink, wrinkled, and rubbery.

She tried to tell them there was nothing to fear when their mother landed on the nest of twigs. The adult robin turned, noticed the little girl, cocked her head in contemplation, and opened her orange beak to speak.

Blip.

A simple, awful sound that took the place of the robin's beautiful singing voice.

Blip.

There was that sound again—mechanical and cold.

Blip.

Blip.

Blip.

The image of the robins and the tree branches contorted and fogged over as the blipping strengthened, becoming as steady as the ticking of a clock.

"No!" she said, looking around. "I want to go back and run with them. I want to sit on the raft with him. I want to look and listen to the birds." Tears ran down her face. "I don't want to go back!"

"Please… please… No…"

Emily opened her eyes. She was in her bedroom, looking at a sight that was all too familiar.

~ * ~

For as long as she could remember, she spent most of her home life in that room. The walls were painted sky blue with overlaid details of various-sized rainbows and clouds.

She had asked for this because she was tired of the bland white walls, she saw every time she returned to the hospital. The dialysis machine stood on the right side of the bed, and an oxygen machine on the left—both hummed and beeped day in and day out. Over time, she had learned to tune out those wearying sounds, but she still knew they were there, a constant reminder of how ill she really was.

Beyond the foot of the bed was a large built-in bookcase that housed her favorite stories she loved to read. The names of Cleary, Dahl, Milne, Baum, Twain, Adams, and Carroll were printed on most of the books.

On the right side of the bookcase was a compact disc stereo system. The speakers were mounted high on the wall. Her music selections were as eclectic as her books. She listened to Mozart, Goodman, Dion, Houston, Brooks, and many others.

Her parents asked if she wanted a television brought into her room so she could watch some shows and movies. She told them she didn't want one. The worlds of books and music gave her such extraordinary dreams that she had no need for anything else. Her imagination helped her escape the room she was in.

Her illness struck when she was four years old. Whatever it was that attacked her body caused her blond hair to fall out, turned her stomach sour, and weakened her arms and legs. She was confined to bed because her legs could no longer support even her frail weight.

In the morning, she would wake up, raise the head of her bed, look out the second-story window, and wait for the sun to rise. She saw clouds pass by in the distance and disappear behind the grand tree in her yard. She dreamt about grabbing onto one of those clouds and floating away from her small world.

What she loved most was the morning rain. She would close her eyes, listening as the drops pounded on the roof and streamed down the gutters into puddles below, letting the smell of rain linger in the air for hours afterward and fill her nose with a fresh, clean scent.

There were mornings when violent winds ripped through the land, slamming against the windows of her room and awakening her. Occasionally, she would watch the rare snowfall drift onto the trees, covering the bare branches with soft fluff. Those were the days her family kept the windows closed.

This morning, as she stared out the window, she noticed something new and bright. She knew it couldn't be the sunlight's reflection—she had memorized everything that appeared in her small window frame of life. She thought she was dreaming of the glowing object that bobbed from side to side, growing larger as it approached her window. She rubbed the sleep from her eyes, looked out the window again, and saw it was still moving closer.

The ball of light positioned itself in the center of the window, absorbing the first rays of the sun. The orb transformed that light into moving colors of blue, red, yellow, purple, orange, and green. A small tear appeared in Emily's eye as she watched the glorious globe move—without resistance—through the glass window and float toward her bed. It rose up and hovered just beyond the reach of her extended, pale fingertips, staying there for a few moments before drifting to the foot of her bed. The colors inside the globe changed; it no longer housed a swirling rainbow but contained a cloud of sad, disturbing gray.

She thought to herself, 'How could this be? How can it change colors and look sad, as if it knows how I feel inside?'

The orb expanded in size, and the colors reappeared. They swirled around inside, increasing to such a speed that her eyes could no longer track even a single color.

With a flash of near-blinding light, a woman stood where the globe once was. She looked at the woman and thought she was one of the most beautiful women she had ever seen, with the exception of her mother.

The woman had pale, bronze-colored skin, rose-red lips, and loosely curled golden-brown hair that stopped around the middle of her back.

She wore a dress made of bright white satin; the sleeves were elbow-length, and the hem fell somewhere below her knees. Emily imagined the bottom of the dress touched the woman's ankles, stopping near her bare feet. On the surface of the dress, the colors flowed throughout, fading in and out. They were the same colors she saw in the globe.

Her eyes were a brilliant green—not an emerald-green, but a deep forest-green. It was the color Emily could see from her bedroom window on the trees' spring leaves. They were very bright and piercing, and Emily felt they touched her soul. She also noticed a deep sadness in those eyes.

Emily wondered why she wasn't afraid of this person or of the way the woman had entered her room. Instead, she felt amazement and peace inside her.

Cautiously, she spoke in a near whisper. "Hello." Her voice had been damaged from years of coughing fits. She couldn't speak without feeling as though her lungs were being torn apart.

The lady replied, "Hello child."

When the woman spoke those two words, the girl could hear faint sounds of wind chimes, falling rain, and singing birds accompanying her voice.

"What is your name, little one?"

"I'm Emily. Some people just call me Em, while others call me Lee."

"And which do you prefer?"

"I like Emily."

"Emily it is then."

"What is your name, Miss?" Emily asked politely.

"What do you think is a good name for me, Emily?"

Emily looked at the woman, studying her. "You look like a rainbow and smell like the rain. Can I call you Rain?"

"Yes. I would be very honored to carry and use that name. Thank you."

"Where did you come from, Rain? I don't know of anyone who can do what you did when you came into my room. That means you must be from elsewhere, right?"

"Yes and no. I am known to come from many places here on Earth. I am from the North, where there is ice everywhere and the cold winds blow unfettered. There, in the mornings, the chill that sharply wakes a person up. When the sun brightly shines upon the land, it looks like a giant sheet of flawless glass as far as the eye can see.

"I am from the South. I have walked the land of the tropics, where there are trees of incredible heights and birds of various shapes and sizes. Some of them have big beaks, while others have giant wingspans. There are some birds so small that they fit on your finger. They have so many voices that when they sing all at once, they sound like a giant orchestra of brass and string instruments.

"I am also from the East, which becomes the West, where a man of ninety years can smile happily as his family grows up around him.

I also come from a place where a child, even younger than you, dies of starvation, sorrow, disease, and war."

Emily sat quietly and listened to Rain. She realized that ever since Rain had come into the room, her coughing had stopped.

"Rain, why are you here now, talking to me?" Emily asked in a voice stronger than she had ever used before. She wanted to ask Rain why her voice was so strong but decided not to risk losing it again.

"I thought you might like some company. I have watched you looking out your window for some time now. You have seen the tree outside your window go through many cycles of life. You have watched as the leaves change from bright green to a multitude of colors, shrivel up, and fall off the branches toward the ground before the cycle begins anew."

"It's always sad to watch that," Emily said, "but I know it will get better when spring arrives, and the sun warms the tree once again."

"You also watch as the ground in the distance change from a spring green to a summer gold, become a wet mess during the fall rains, and then get covered in a coat of white snow when winter arrives."

"I have seen the snow," Emily said, "but have never touched it. My windows are always closed for most of that time of year."

"That is another reason I am here. I have come to show you places which you have only dreamed of. If you like, I can and will make it real for you."

"How can you show me these places when I can't move my legs? How can I hear the sounds you speak of when the birds begin to sing, and I then interrupt them with my coughing? I am always so sick. I cannot leave my bed to go with you to see and hear those things. I hurt all the time."

Rain's eyes began to well up, and tears streaked down her face.

Sometimes I feel like I just want to give up, but I don't. If there is even a small chance to get better, I want that to happen for me and my family. It's so hard to put on a happy face for my family, knowing that it may never happen, and I hope that it would all end—the pain, the sadness, the tears, and the lies we tell each other to keep our hopes up."

Rain spoke. "You have become more tired and frail as the seasons roll on. However, no matter how much you hurt, you have tried to smile. That is why I came to you.

"I have seen your mother come into your room smiling but looking worn and tear streaked. I have seen her strength worsen as she worries about you more every day."

"When she leaves your room, she heads for her small corner of the house where your father cannot see her. She holds a little doll you once held, rocking back and forth in that corner while speaking to herself quietly. 'How can this be happening? Why is she dying? What is taking my little girl's life so slowly, so painfully? Did I cause this? Is this a punishment? If so, why hurt my little girl? Why not hurt me instead? Why, why, why?'"

Emily spoke as her tears fell. "I've heard her crying for hours. She wants to know why my life is being taken away. I don't know what to say to her anymore. Sometimes I wish all of this were over. My mom's grief may have ended by now and started over with my dad. I've always wanted a brother or a sister. Maybe she would feel better if she thought of me in a better place, instead of seeing me day after day stuck in this body."

"Who could do this to my family? Why do they want to destroy us?" Emily's face was now red and wet with tears of anger and grief.

"One thing has done this to you," Rain said, "and that is Death. Sometimes It comes so slowly that you can feel your life being gradually drained from you no matter how hard you fight to stay alive.

"Death can also be quick, brutal, and so harsh that It takes life away in just a moment—with a snap of Its' fingers—and then carries them to the next Realm that they dreamt and believed in."

Rain exhaled and spoke with some care in her voice, "There are times when Death does care about what happens to those who are near passing on. It does not want them to suffer the pains of a tortured life. It can feel their pain and wants to help them and by ending their suffering, but something holds Them back from doing so.

"It is the hope of that person thinking and willing themselves to hold onto life just a little bit longer, no matter the pain they are in.

"Their thoughts can also keep them here, thinking, 'If I can make it to another day, I will be able to walk, laugh, go to school, and grow up.'"

Emily commented, "I would like to go to school and to be with other kids. I want to learn everything the teachers can teach me."

Rain sat down beside Emily. "If you like, I could be your teacher. I could show you everything that you would ever want to see, hear, and touch. There is so much beauty that you would lose yourself in it. The world would bow to you as it does to me. You would be able to see all of Man's creations and destructions. You would also see what they will make in the future."

"If I do leave, what would happen to my mom and my dad? Won't they be sad that I am gone?"

Rain lowered her head and nodded. "Yes, they will be. I will not lie to you. They will also know that you will be in a better place than the one that exists now. For the first time, you could be genuinely happy. You would be able to walk, run, and laugh. You could even sing with the birds as loud as you would like, until you exhaust the air in your lungs. And when you catch your breath, you could start again. Come with me, little one. Let us escape this place that surrounds you and tortures you. Say yes and take the next step with me, Emily."

I know it's my time," Emily said. "I have spent my life in bed like this, watching myself waste away." She slowly sat up in her bed. "Yes, please. I want to see, run, and do everything I can't do now. I am willing to move on from here."

"Take hold of my hand and let us move on. You will be able to see the world, forever free from any of the boundaries you now have." Rain extended her long, elegant fingers to Emily. "I promise you will no longer feel the pains of your past."

Emily took Rain's hand, smiled, and braced herself against the woman. She slid her feet out from under the covers, off the side of her bed, and placed them firmly on the floor. She evaluated the strength of her legs with her body weight, fearful that she might crumble on the spot.

They did not disappoint her. She took a few steps forward and then a few steps back. She released her grip on Rain, started spinning in place, and laughed like the little girl she was meant to be.

After a minute, she stopped, walked up to the Rain, wrapped her tiny arms around her, and gave her a hug. Rain leaned down and kissed her lightly on the top of her head. They separated and turned toward the window. A smile crossed Emily's lips as she and Rain walked into the expanding sunlight, hand in hand.

Chapter Two - Jeremy

Downtown Chicago,

late July.

The temperatures reached the upper nineties that week. Humidity remained in the upper seventies, and the residents of the city were practically breathing and drinking the air.

The air was stagnant; the moisture inside the sewer systems heated up and released a noxious odor that settled at street level. The heat caused the walls to sweat, with dripping grime and car exhaust.

During those days of no rain and hazy skies, the name "Windy City" did not seem to fit Chicago and its surrounding communities.

The people of the Chicago metroplex found various ways to try and stay cool. They closed their windows and turned on their air conditioners. The overuse of central air and small personal units placed a strain on the electrical grid, creating rolling blackouts and brownouts that stifled their temporary respite from the heat.

They drank an inordinate amount of alcohol, which gave them the illusion of staying hydrated and cool.

Some found themselves in or near water. They lounged poolside, took a dip in the deep end, or just decided to get their feet wet. Others walked the lakefront, hoping for a rogue breeze of air to cross over cooler waters and provide a few moments of relief from the unrelenting, pounding hazed sun. There were those who took extreme measures to escape those heated days—days filled with stagnant air smells, blaring street noises of horns and vocal cursing—and to help dampen their inner demonic voices that believed life is God's own personal cruel joke to Himself. Jeremy was one of those people.

~ * ~

He entered a Chicago hospital at ten thirty-seven P.M. by ambulance. While in the emergency room, the doctors and nurses removed his clothing at a hostile rate. Jeremy was in cardiac arrest.

After his clothing was torn and cut from his torso and arms, they noticed deep bluish-purple markings in several places on his arms.

Jeremy could barely understand what the people around him were saying as he slipped in and out of drug-hazed consciousness.

"Caucus… Brown ha… Brown eye... Six… two… One… Eighty-fi… twenty years old."

He was twenty years old. He was too old to be considered a teenager, someone who hangs out in the school's parking lot smoking, drinking, and flirting instead of going to class—yet too young to go into bars and clubs to drink without being carded or removed from the premises.

Jeremy was in that transitional phase of becoming a man: his beard was thickening, his facial features were lengthening, and the final spurts of growth were taking effect.

The gurney shifted, giving him a jolt and bouncing around. Overhead, he saw rolling shadows and lights behind his closed eyelids. He believed he was being pushed through a bright tunnel.

Then the gurney halted.

He could feel the breathing of many individuals above him. His body trembled violently. He felt hands emerging from the darkness of his mind, touching him from every direction.

12

A scream of panic escaped his body without his consent.

He felt more hands.

Hands all around.

Heavy breathing from the darkness came at him from all around.

Hot hands touching. Fiery breaths on his skin.

Hot breaths! Burning hands!

Screams were coming from everywhere!

Screams coming from himself!

An overwhelming emptiness filled his mind as the burning touches and fiery breaths disappeared.

There in the darkness, Jeremy felt a solitary set of hands that he focused on. They were cool and… silky. He felt them brush over his chest, and his inner trembles began to fade away.

A voice pierced through his mental haze. "Shh. Calm down. Everything will be fine." The voice had a strange tone to it. To Jeremy, there was a sound accompanying her voice, like wind chimes made of seashells. "You shouldn't be shaking anymore."

"I'm unable to see anything. Why?"

"It is just a side effect of your withdrawal."

Jeremy smelled a familiar scent in the air. "Did it start raining earlier?"

"It has not rained as of yet."

"Then why does it feel cooler?"

"We are in the lower levels. It is cooler there," she said, as if it were unimportant information. "Do you want me to call you Jeremy or J.C?"

"How did you know my name?"

"I got your name from your wallet."

"Oh. Call me Jeremy. My parents call me J.C. I really hate that name."

 Fine. Jeremy it is then."

"What's your name?"

"I have been going by Rain recently because of a young lady I met on my travels. I carry the name because of her."

"That sounds like a rad name to me. I'm going to bet you got a lot of tattoos?"

"No." She spoke a single word so harsh that it froze Jeremy's blood.

"So, when will I be able to see again?"

"You will be able to see after a while. You need to give it a little time."

"Well, that's good to know. At least I won't have to walk around with a cane, asking for money."

Rain sighed. "Most people with a disability do not stand around begging or asking for charity. They face their disability with courage and maybe a bit of hope. They believe their disability allows them to see the world differently."

"Yeah. Sure. Whatever," Jeremy said, ignoring her words. "You should see them all hanging around the country club my family goes to—beggars, blind men, retards, and even gimps. They all want a handout. It's all funny if you ask me."

Irritated with Jeremy's attitude and comments, Rain decided to change the conversation. "Why would you want to destroy your body with all those drugs you put inside you? I can see the marks, the blemishes, and the grayness. They run deep into your skin and deep inside of you."

"It's all about the rush, pure and simple. It's not a question of addiction for me. I use so I can feel nothing and care about nothing."

"When did it start for you?"

"You sound like you're doing a report."

"In a way, I guess I am. I hope you do not mind?" Rain replied.

"It's not a problem." Jeremy paused and searched his thoughts. "Let me see. I started having beer parties at my house when I was fourteen. My friends and I partied all day long since my parents were never home.

"My mom is a big-time city prosecutor. All she worries about is getting the criminals off Chicago's streets. She's either my father's third or fourth wife, I can't remember which. She had me late in life because she was focused on her career. Once I was old enough to be placed in the care of nannies, babysitters, or daycare centers, she returned her focus to her job.

"And my father. My father's a college professor. He teaches English Literature. He always speaks in 'proper tongue.' My father was also a sixties activist. He used to talk about all the changes they were going to make in America—and how stoned he was during Woodstock.

"If you think that I'm going to blame them for what I do, you're wrong. For the past five years, I've seen them barely ten or twelve times.

"Hell, my friends and I would party at one person's house one night, then go to another house the next day. After a while, we went to my place more often since there was no threat of my parents coming home and busting us. We'd get our older friends to go buy the alcohol. They'd get us cases of beer, bottles of Jack, schnapps, Tito's— anything else we wanted. I had the run of the basement. My parents would never come downstairs. They said they wanted to respect my privacy.

"Anyway, a few of my friends invited more friends than usual one night. I had never met these guys before, but they seemed cool. They started drinking and talking to me and my people.

One of the new guys pulled out a bag of white powder, and I said, 'Is that coke?' He nodded. I asked if I could try some, and he said, 'Go ahead and help yourself.' Some of my friends and I did a few lines, sat down, and tripped out.

"I'm not going to describe to you my trip—or any other trips— because they were mine. I don't know how I got to my bedroom that night. All I know is that my mind and body was juiced, and I wanted more.

"I continued doing coke through the rest of high school. I'd get home from school, start to drink, and do some lines from four until nine. Then I would go to my room and stay there until the sun came up. Sometimes I would stay there until many suns came up. My parents never questioned me about my after-school activities. I still don't know how much they know about my life."

Jeremy realized his vision was slowly returning. He looked toward Rain and saw a fuzzy image of the nurse. He sat up, let his legs swing off the side of the gurney, closed his eyes because the light was hurting them, and continued his story.

"Around six months ago, the guys I get my coke from said they had something even more powerful than coke without making you paranoid after taking it and it would cost less. I thought that was great because I was already snorting a lot, and my parents were questioning about things that were missing from the house. I wanted something new.

"Out of nowhere, they pulled out a needle. Let me just say, if I were anywhere near sober, they wouldn't have even brought that needle near me. But, of course, I wasn't sober. They tied off my arm for the free sample and put it in me.

"When they released the band from my arm, I could feel the pure fire in my veins. After that, the world no longer existed for me and believe you me, that was about it."

"Again, why would you do what you do to yourself?" Rain asked.

Take a long look around. This entire world is as black as night. I like looking at the world in my own way. I can control my own actions and not let the world decide where I'm going."

When Jeremy finished his story, his sight cleared up. He looked Rain up and down. He saw that she had bronze skin, golden hair, and a body he would kill for just to touch. She wore a white nursing outfit with a pin on her collar that looked like a rainbow. What interested him the most were her eyes. They were a cold, harsh green.

"For being a nurse, you sure do look good. How about you and me going out after I get out of this place later? I can tell you a lot more about myself."

She stood up and moved toward the door. "I'm sorry, but I do not date any of my clients. Besides, I have the information I wanted, so this is where we will part. Thank you for your answers. They have been quite illuminating, to say the very least."

"Hey! Where do you think you're going?" Jeremy asked, his tone indicating he hadn't dismissed her yet. He laid his hand on her shoulder and gripped her arm.

Rain stopped in her tracks, turned toward him causing his hand to slip off and gave him a look of annoyance. "Who are you to question me?!" she demanded, her voice no longer carrying the gentle sound of chimes but instead the harsh ring of crushing metal. "How dare you speak or touch me in any way after what you did tonight?!"

"What did I do?"

"You almost killed them! You passed out and slammed your car into a group of children by the museum. Two of them are still in a coma! I do not know which way their lives will move as of yet."

"I'll get my parents to take care of that after I get out of here. They've taken care of some of my other problems before."

I do not think you understand what is going on. You are not getting out of here. You are dead—you died at the end of telling your story to me. I did not want to tell you in case I decided to return you to the physical world, deeming you worthy enough. But since you have been here, you have not shown me any hint that you would change. Do you know why you did what you did when it came to drugs and alcohol? You have never felt anything, even before it all began. You prejudged the world you live in and decided it was not worth your time to make a difference. Even now, all you have done is act pompous and arrogant. Therefore, I consider you a suicide and invoke the penalty that you assuredly deserve."

"And what would that be? Am I to be a civil servant of the dead?" Jeremy asked in a ragged, stuttered, meek voice.

"That only happens in the movies. You will feel the pain you caused your body at the moment of its death. You will feel the hot, lethal poison being inserted into your arm. You will feel it as it rises through your veins, burning throughout your body. Then you will feel your heart explode in your chest. Finally, you will feel your brain hemorrhage as it starves for oxygen."

"After that cycle is completed, it will all begin once again for each shot that you gave yourself. When your punishment is complete, Suicide Death will slowly absorb your body into itself, and you will be no more—no afterlife and no reincarnation. You will cease to exist, forever."

Jeremy began to shake from fear as he cried out, "Why are you doing this to me?"

Rain said, as she exited the door, "I did nothing to you, but you know who did." With no more to say, she left without looking back. The door closed on the whimpering young man.

Jeremy heard a noise coming from underneath the floor, it sounded like something was trying to break through. Jeremy screamed and shuffled into the nearest corner of the room, huddled like an infant and watched as it tore a hole through the floor. It crawled out, then stood on its legs, moving toward him.

It was like nothing Jeremy could ever have imagined.

Its fleshy skull bore numerous piercing bullet holes. The neck showed multiple knife slices and abrasions from ropes and cloths. The skin on its arms displayed a combination of cuts and deep, dark needle marks. Its chest had gaping holes from bullets, shells, and other impacts. What remained of its skin was the color of black cinder, with putrid red, caked-on blood from the multiple wounds it had acquired over the centuries.

Jeremy's last thought, as he went into convulsions, was, "I did this to myself."

Chapter Three - Nicky

Nicky stared into the living room from the corner of the hallway. He remained motionless, watching as the stranger in the black mask slapped his mother with the gun.

"Okay, bitch. Where's the money?"

"I don't have any! My husband left and took it all," Becky cried out, as traces of blood trickled out from between her lips.

The man grabbed her matted copper hair with his unarmed hand and turned her face toward him. "I don't believe you. Now tell me where the fuck the money is before I hurt that pretty face again."

"I don't have anything!"

The man struck her face again.

A droplet of blood leaped from Becky's lips and landed on the tip of Nicky's footed blue bunny pajamas. He watched as it absorbed into the cloth.

The man let Becky go and continued searching the living room. He stormed around, smashing anything within his reach.

Against the north wall stood a wooden bookcase. He threw the books, papers, and other baubles off the shelves, looking behind them for some sort of hidden spot.

On the south wall sat the couch and a picture window. The window shades were drawn for the night. He looked under the seats and around the frame of the couch but found nothing.

On the east wall stood what remained of the oak front door. A hole surrounded the edges where the deadbolt used to be.

The west wall contained various pictures and a television set. The entrance to the hallway was on that wall.

Upset, the man shoved his foot into the television. The tube exploded outward into the living room. A shard of glass struck Becky on the cheek. She flinched from the cut and turned her head toward the hallway.

That's when she noticed Nicky for the first time. Panic and terror surged through her bloodstream, sending chills from her fingertips to her toenails. Her body trembled from the adrenaline. Her red eyes widened in fear.

She whispered to her son, "Go back to your room and be really quiet." She closed her eyes, took a shaky breath, then reopened them, refocusing on Nicky. "Don't let him hear you. Go. Now." Her voice shook with the horrible thought of Nicky being hurt by the man.

The man heard her, turned to the right, and looked directly at Nicky. "Com'mere kid. I wanna talk to you. Your mom's being a bitch. She won't tell me anything, but you will, won'tcha?" He moved forward to grab him.

Nicky stumbled backward and ran down the hallway, passing the kitchen on his right.

The man lunged after him, but Becky blocked his path.

She was bruised, bloody, and her cheeks were stained with tears. She felt ready to pass out from the pain, but she stood her ground to protect her child. He was everything to her.

She screamed at him, "Don't touch him, you bastard! Leave him alone!" Then, she took a roundhouse swing.

The punch struck him in the face, but he didn't flinch. With his left hand, he grabbed her. He raised his gun, pressed it against her forehead, and pulled the trigger twice.

A jolt. The sound of explosions filled the house, echoing through the hallway.

~*~

Nicky heard his mother shriek before two loud bangs and then heard something landing on the floor hard. He was so afraid that all he wanted to do was run safely into his mother's arms—but she was back where the noises came from.

With Him.

He ran into his bedroom, frantically searching for something. It wasn't found on the table, or the dresser. He found the small, round plastic container under his bed.

He removed the lid, reached inside, and pulled the item out. Standing up, he turned toward the door.

The man was there.

He was a giant compared to Nicky. His head nearly touched the top of the doorway, and his shoulders brushed the sides. In one hand, he held the weapon he had used on Nicky's mother. In the other, a clump of hair dangled between his fingers.

Nicky slowly raised his small hand, palm up. "Here's my money. Don't hurt my mommy anymore."

Resting on his outstretched palm, Nicky held a shiny new quarter.

The man raised the gun at Nicky and pulled back the hammer. Nicky peered into the gun's chamber. Then, he heard the same noise from earlier.

He saw something small move down the gun's passageway. The whole room darkened slowly.

The man lowered the gun, turned around, and left the room without looking back.

There, on the floor, lay the quarter near Nicky's head.

~*~

The massive, black-shadowed figure left Nicky's room. A small, dim nightlight in the far corner cast a faint glow. The light reflected off the coin on the floor.

Nicky picked up the quarter. His small hand tightened around it as he slowly stood up. The house was silent. He wanted to go down the hallway to find his mom, but fear held him back. "Mommy?" he whispered. "Mommy, are you there?"

No answer.

From behind him, the light grew brighter—but it wasn't coming from the nightlight. Nicky turned around and stared as a circular spot of light expanded, growing taller and wider before his eyes.

Someone stepped out from the center of the glowing circle. A woman stood there. Her dress absorbed the light and began to glow, as if woven from a combination of brightest of white and wisps of colors from a rainbow.

The light of the dress reflected off her golden hair and bronze skin. She knelt on one knee and opened her arms wide toward Nicky.

"Come here, little one. I will protect you from the darkness and return you to the light."

"Where's Mommy?" Nicky asked.

"I will take you to where she is if you come along with me." She kept her voice calm to soothe him. She could tell it was working. He moved toward her as she continued speaking. "Climb into my arms, and I will carry you to a place where we can find her. I promise."

"Okay. Take me there." He paused, remembering his manners. "Please."

Nicky moved cautiously toward Rain. She picked him up, tightened her grip, and gave him a comforting hug.

Without knowing why, he felt safe in the lady's arms. He felt like no one could hurt him when she held him. Nicky also noticed that she smelled nice—like clean water.

As she carried Nicky through his room, Rain briefly covered his eyes as they were leaving. Fear gripped him for a moment, but she released his eyes in the hallway.

"Why did you cover my eyes?" he asked.

"I did not want you to see the terrible things the man did in there. I am sorry—I should have told you what I was going to do."

He nodded in acceptance.

As they moved down the hallway, Rain asked, "Nicky, can I cover your eyes again, okay? I do not want you to be afraid. I promise. I will not hurt you, but I do not want you to look either."

"Okay, lady."

"Call me Rain."

"Okay, Rain." He buried his head into Rain's chest.

Rain stepped into the entrance of the living room—a memory built from Nicky's vision.

On the north wall stood an empty wooden bookcase. The books lay scattered across the floor.

The window shades on the south wall were down. The couch was knocked over, and its cushions disorganized.

On the east wall stood what remained of the oak front door. A jagged piece of wood hung from the metal deadbolt, barely clinging to the wall. The door itself was splintered in multiple places—from the intruder kicking his foot into it.

The west wall held crooked, askew pictures, and the television's tube had been shattered by the stranger's boot. Rain surmised that had been his first weapon of choice.

She viewed the room from Nicky's perspective, seeing the image of Becky. She saw the bruises left by the blows, the split lip, and moved to where Nicky had stood.

Becky was staring directly at Rain, repeating the final words she had said to Nicky before turning to confront the intruder. Rain made sure that the sound was muted to Nicky, shielding him from hearing what she was watching.

The intruder was an overwhelming sight. He towered over Becky, his form a black, ever-growing shadow that stretched from wall to wall, creeping into every corner of the room.

As the moment replayed from the point where Nicky ran down the hallway, Rain heard a guttural scream rising from deep within the blackness.

At the moment Becky was shot, she and the room were completely enveloped in darkness. The noise of the shots created a concussive effect, echoing off Rain and down the darkening hallway.

What felt like both a lifetime and mere moments passed. A small light flickered around Nicky's doorway before fading into blackness, accompanied by another concussive wave.

Then, light returned, and the room reset—beginning the ending tale once again.

"How many times did you have to live through this, little one?" she said in horror.

~*~

She took Nicky to the kitchen entrance in the hallway. "Hold on, this will only tingle for a second."

A bright gate appeared in front of Rain, and she stepped through with Nicky. A small ticklish giggle escaped from him. 'That was a good sign,' she thought. "Okay, you can look now."

He turned his head to see where they were. Above him, a blue sky stretched wide, fluffy white clouds bobbing along with a gentle breeze pushing them. Below, a dirt path wound between neatly groomed grass on both sides.

Rain placed him down on the path, and he looked further ahead. In the distance, children played in a vast field surrounded by more grass, bushes, and small trees. Some peeked around the edges in a game of hide-and-seek, while others dangled from the lower branches of the trees by their arms and legs.

As the two of them approached, a few children paused their play and ran over. They wrapped their arms around Rain's waist and then extended their hands to Nicky in greeting.

Rain knelt. "I would like for you to stay here for a while, Nicky. There is water to drink, food to eat, and if you would like, you can talk to the birds. The others would love it if you played with them, or you could sit under a tree."

"I want my mommy."

A girl with blonde hair, a gold dress, and bare feet said, "I promise you, Nicky, that's exactly what Rain is going to do. She will bring her to you. If you like, you could be It for a little while she goes and gets your mom. How does that sound?"

Nicky grinned and ran in the direction of the others, who took off, knowing the game was back on.

~*~

27

Rain walked in the opposite direction down the path, away from the children. She arrived at an area where the path cut through a region of tall, breeze-blown wheatgrass and waited there.

A young woman in her twenties stepped out of the field. She was a full head shorter than Rain, with deep brown hair and naturally tan skin.

"Greetings, I am Rain. I believe you were told to walk through the grass and that you would meet someone who would take you to your son?"

"I don't think I was told that. I just had a feeling to go in a certain direction to find my son and get my questions answered. So where am I, and why is Nicky here?"

"This is a starting place to help reunite those who have lost each other. I watch over a Place that allows me to care for the children until their mothers and fathers claim them. You and Nicky had a tragic experience, and he has been waiting for you."

"Since the shooting, you were in a coma for some time before your time ended."

"Has Nicky been here that whole time?"

"No. He was in a place of his own making. The fear and violence of your experience affected his safe passage here. He was lost in an endless loop of that incident for some time. I stepped in when I had the opportunity and brought him here."

"How long is 'some time'?"

"It is ever-changing. He could have been there for only moments yet found himself replaying that cycle multiple times. When I was there, the story happened three times at different speeds. He has been here since, and that nightmare is all but gone from his memory now."

"This place is a little like Neverland. The bad memories are washed away after a time, leaving only laughter, joyous claps," Rain smirked— "and maybe a couple of faeries flying around for the fun of it."

"And what of my memories?"

"The next Place will take care of that. Come now. Nicky has been waiting for you to come and collect him."

Rain returned to the play area with Becky in hand. As they approached the group of children, Becky released her hand from Rain's and moved toward them.

She had only taken ten steps when she saw Nicky. He was wearing shorts, a loose t-shirt, and no shoes, running around chasing the other children.

When he saw his mother, he turned and galloped over. Becky grabbed him and pulled him into a bear hug. Her eyes were wet with joy as she held her child.

"Thank you, Rain. Thank you for finding and watching over my son."

"You are quite welcome. I wish you nothing but the best in the next Place."

"Can I ask you something?"

"Of course."

"What happened to the man who did this to us?"

"His life came to an end a short while later," Rain said. "After the incident, he went off, got drunk, and then overdrank, trying to erase the guilt of the shooting and the last image of Nicky while he was alive. He could do neither, so he decided to walk into a moving semi-truck.

"

"At this time, and for a long time to come, one of my associates is handling him. Do not worry, his treatment will not be the same as yours. They deal in the punishment of those who cause pain and death."

"Now, it is time for you to leave and go where you belong. Your pain is over. As you continue further down this path there will be a large tree of green and gold. Walk to its base and into the shadow. It will take you to a Place you dreamed of and prayed for."

The mother pulled Rain close in a hug. "Thank you so very much. I will not forget you."

She and Nicky turned away and started down the path Rain had pointed out. They stopped for a moment. Nicky whispered something into his mother's ear, then climbed out of her arms and headed toward Rain.

He stopped in front of her, reached into his pocket, pulled something out, and dropped it into Rain's hand. Then, he ran back to his mother, and they continued down the path until they disappeared from Rain's sight.

She looked down at her hand to see what he had given her. Tears welled in her eyes, and she smiled when she saw what lay in her palm.

It was the shiny, new quarter.

Chapter Four - Mara

As the first light of the sun illuminated the eastern horizon, slipping between two towers, it caught a glimpse of Mara, a young lady dressed in a rose-colored half-slip, and barefooted. Her long, thin brown hair whipped around her face in the whistling winds that twisted around her.

She stood at the edge of the twelve-story building, bending her right knee and dipping her left foot below the roof's edge. She was calculating how long it would take to hit the ground below.

Mara was tired, alone, and distraught. Her face was raw from the wind and from wiping away her tears with trembling hands. The remnants of black mascara and eyeshadow were hideously smeared across her eyes and cheeks.

"HE LIED TO ME!" she screamed, staring at the ground. "THE BASTARD SAID FOREVER! FOREVER IS NOT NOW!"

Mara turned her head skyward. She saw the last reflection of multicolored hues in the otherwise white clouds, the colors of the day overtaking the deep purple of dawn's early light.

"ARE YOU LAUGHING AT ME UP THERE? POOR LITTLE MARA, TRICKED BY THE BASTARD! WHY DON'T YOU JUST FUCK YOURSEL—"

Her last word was canceled out by a sudden gust of wind that nearly pushed her over the edge. It swept her unsteady legs out from under her, and she fell onto her right shoulder, rolling toward the drop.

With a quick intake of air, she deftly caught the ledge with her left hand. She hung there for a moment before moving her right hand up to the safe side of the ledge. Digging her toes into the brick wall, she pulled herself back over the edge.

Once safe on the solid surface, she sat down. Her entire body shook from her fingertips to her toenails. Each breath sent a shiver through her. She turned her head upward again.

"Don't be so impatient. I'll get there soon enough." She whispered while exhaling.

She closed her eyes and brushed her hair from her face, only for the wind to whip it back again.

Opening her eyes, she moved forward to watch the world below. The streets showed only a few people and two buses passing beside each other. No one down there seemed to notice her as they carried on with their daily business.

Then, the street below blurred. Mara wiped at her eyes, expecting tears, but finding there were none—even though her vision remained unfocused.

The blur rippled, as if a stone had been dropped into a clear lake. In the center of the ripples, images began to form. She saw herself and others—viewed through the eyes of someone else.

She saw herself on her fourth birthday, burning her finger on one of her own birthday candles. An image of her mother dressing her in heavy clothes for a trek outside, only to have to remove them all again so she could go to the bathroom. Her mother looked exasperated but had a gleam of laughter in her eyes.

Then, different images of Rusty appeared at the center of the ripple effect she was peering into.

Rusty was not his real name, but his copper-red hair gave Mara the idea to call him that, and the nickname stuck. Since their first year of junior high, Rusty had always been by her side. He was there to help—or cheat—on homework assignments.

He helped her get around when she broke her leg dodging a mad bee. Rusty was there for her first kiss. He was the only boy she had ever kissed or been intimate with.

The image shifted forward in time.

She was standing by the school lockers when she heard some girls talking on the other side.

"How was your date?" one girl asked.

"Satisfying."

"Where did he take you?"

"The Bistro over on Sixth Street."

"Romantic. What happened next?"

"He took me to the movies."

"Which one?"

"I really don't remember. We made out the whole time, until the movie was way over."

The girls laughed and made kissing sounds into the air.

"And then he snuck me into his bedroom, where we fucked for hours. I didn't make it home until after 1 A.M. My mom almost caught me."

Mara smiled, thinking of Rusty and the time they had spent together making love.

"Lucky. So, have you talked to him yet today?"

"No, not yet. John said that Rusty would---".

Those were the last words Mara heard before she crumbled to the ground.

~*~

Tears welled in Mara's eyes. "Nooo… Why?"

She reached for the image of her crushed self. As the tips of her fingers neared it, the image shifted, turning into a black tar-like substance. She quickly pulled her hand away.

Inside the image, the blackness morphed into a new image, a human looking creature made of bone and of torn cloth. The edges of the rippled vision expanded, and the being grew larger with it.

The skeletal figure opened its cloak, revealing an eternal abyss of nothingness.

"Leap to me. You can do it. Just one step more. You can join me and my companion."

The voice was snake-like, distinctly female, and was accompanied by a choir of guttural moans that filled Mara's ears and thoughts of dread. The creature's bony hands released the cloak's edge, extended it toward Mara, and reaching beyond the confines of the screen.

"Come, Mara."

Mara stumbled further back onto the blacktop of the building. She staggered to her feet, stepping further away.

"Who's your companion? Where are they?"

Panic and fear paralyzed her, locking her in place before the deathly apparition.

The empty eye socket of the skeletal figure expanded, growing until it consumed the entire screen. Then, the image lunged forward, engulfing Mara from head to toe in a cold, thick darkness.

A soul-chilling gust of air rushed past her ears, whipping her hair back.

A dull yellow glow surrounded the image as it expanded from the black depths. Though it made no movement, the distance between them closed, until Mara was nearly face to face with the horrible sight.

The creature's face was a mangled mess. Torn swatches of what could only be considered clothing hung precariously from its twisted, shredded skin and protruding, broken, contorted bones.

Every burn, rip, tear, and fractured bone told Mara exactly how each mark, tear, crack, and fracture had been made—the self-inflictions of others upon themselves.

It raised what remained of its hand and touched Mara's left shoulder, sending a searing wave of flame and acid down her arm and into her fingertips.

A gut-wrenching scream tore from Mara's body as she staggered back, recoiling from it.

Mara fell from the darkness and landed back on the concrete roof of the building.

The bone-and-cloth specter stood guard at the entrance of the void from which Mara had escaped. The boned creature's front remained eerily still, unwavering, but behind it, flowing strips of cloth melded with the void as if they were one. Some of its fabric extended and retracted in multiple directions.

Mara feared the fabric would reach out, seize her, and drag her back into the darkness trapping her in the blackness forever.

Then, another female figure emerged from the place where the creature stood guard, passing through the guardian of the void unfettered.

She was a golden-brown-haired woman with pale-bronzed skin and deep green eyes, wearing a dress as white as the rising sun. Within the fabric, a multitude of colors flowed, shifting within the cloth's confines.

The woman strode toward Mara with confidence. Stopping just short of her, she extended her hand and said, "My name is Rain, and I am here to help you rise above this moment."

Mara stood up while her eyes focused on the dark figure behind this woman, searching for any sign of movement. "Who, or what, is that behind you?" Mara asked, trepidation in her voice.

Rain turned to face the dark image at the edge of the building. She stood still for a moment, observing it, then slowly circled around the figure, studying it from all angles.

"This is an image of fear," Rain said. She swiped her hand through the creature and the void, both dissipating into nothingness. "And of selfishness."

She turned back toward Mara.

"Who... or what are you?" Mara asked, taking a deep breath, her eyes wide.

"As I have said, I am Rain."

"What kind of fear and selfishness would create something like that?" Mara asked, pointing to the space where the image had been.

"The selfishness of believing the world revolves around them, convinced that no one would care if they disappeared. The fear is of an uncertain future—where the unknown and loneliness frighten a person so much that they no longer wish to continue living."

"That would be waiting for me if I jump?"

"Yes," she stated with absolution. "The boned one would take you and escort you to the other, who would, in turn, consume you into itself."

Mara gasped, took a step back, and lost all feeling in her legs. She fell heavily onto her lower backside.

She brought her closed fist to her lips, closed her eyes, and let the tears fall. "I just want this pain to go away. It hurts so much."

Rain bent down to meet Mara's gaze. "Do you think so little of yourself that you would throw away all that you have learned—and all that you will learn in the times to come—because of that boy?"

"You are still a child in this world. That boy, too, is still a child. He is not your soul, he is not in your blood, and he does not make your spirit soar.

"Your soul is deep within you. Your blood courses through your veins and makes you stronger. Your spirit soars by living and loving life every day that you can, for you are precious. You are needed in this world.

"By doing what you are thinking of doing, you do not become a martyr of love. You become just another statistic of Death."

With that, Rain leaned down and kissed the top of Mara's head. A passing breeze brushed a few strands of Mara's hair in assistance.

Rain stood with the grace of a swan, her back to the rising sun. "You have been touched by Death but not kissed. This is an opportunity few can claim to have survived or moved on from. I hope for something different from you—something truly magnificent that will make a difference, not only in your life but in the lives of those you love."

Stepping backward into the surrounding sunlight, Rain's dress flowed, touched, and melded with the light—then she was gone.

Mara sat and watched as the sun rose above the buildings before her.

She felt the heat of the day as the sun passed overhead.

She felt the chill on her shoulders as the sun settled behind her.

When the last of the sunlight faded and the colors of the day dissipated, she stood.

She wiped away whatever tears remained on her face, turned, and headed toward the building's exit.

Chapter Five - Kathryn

Three months since the funeral.

Three months of sleepless nights and late mornings.

Countless days without an appetite and continuous, heart-wrenching grief housed inside her chest.

Since the day of their daughter's death, Kathryn and her husband, Alex, had been sleeping in separate beds. Each night, she climbed into her daughter's small medical bed, curled up with her ragdoll, and stared out the large bay windows.

She had failed to be there with her daughter in the end to hold her hand, to say it would be all right. To watch over her while she slept. To hear her last breath and catch that one final smile she would remember for long as she should live.

Kathryn and her husband spoke less and less. She believed he didn't care about their daughter's passing. She lashed out at him, accusing him of being emotionless. She asked why he couldn't bring himself to cry on that first day, or throughout the funeral.

When they spoke, they argued. She tried to goad him into verbal fights just to see if he could show some emotion.

Any emotion.

He explained that he wanted to be strong for both of them. She refused to listen, accusing him of lying to her. To her, it was just another excuse to avoid the truth that everything had ended the day their daughter's death.

He wanted to go to counseling to work through their issues. She didn't want to leave the house. He offered to bring the counselors to their home. She refused to let anyone through the door.

"They are only trying to help us heal. We need help."

"No! You need help. I just want our daughter back. If they can't do that, then they can't help. They can't feel what I feel in my chest. All I feel is the overwhelming pain in my heart. I need her to calm my heart. I need to feel her breath and her heartbeat in my arms."

Kathryn stormed away and slammed the door to their daughter's bedroom.

She locked the door behind her as she entered the room, then moved to the corner closest to the window and the bed. Leaning against the edges of the corner for support, she slid down into a ball and cried until she could cry no more.

She stared at the little bed, where a pillow and a throw blanket lay on top. On the floor, scattered photographs of her shattered family lay strewn about.

"She's gone. Gone, gone, gone," the voice in Kathryn's mind whispered. "How could she have left me? How could I have left her side that day? The machines said she had just stopped. There was no shallow breathing to sound the alarms. There was no alert of her heartbeat elevating or slowing. She just… stopped."

Kathryn stood, moved to the side of the bed, and gripped it with both hands.

"Why did you stop?" she screamed aloud, flipping the bed so hard it slammed against the wall near the door. "Why?"

A crushing pain erupted inside her chest and raced down her arms.

Her knees buckled, and she dropped to the floor.

Her hands curled inward, clutching her chest. Her breathing became strangled, and her vision blurred.

She forced out a single word through her lips. "Alex."

As her vision darkened, she heard a crack from the doorframe, followed by the door slamming against the bed as it was thrown open.

The last thing she saw was her husband reaching for her.

~*~

Kathryn caught her breath, steadying her nerves as she opened her eyes.

What she saw was neither her husband nor her daughter's disheveled bedroom. She was seated on a white-illuminated path, staring into a black void ahead.

She turned to her left and saw the path darkening further down the lane, the light gradually becoming extinguished beyond her sight.

Turning her head to the right, she saw the path glowing brightly, leading toward an arching gate of light that warded off the surrounding darkness.

She stood and walked toward the brighter direction of the path.

As Kathryn continued along, fuzzy images began to appear atop the voids on both sides. They reminded her of the white sheets her family used to hang outside to watch movies in the dead of night. The longer she looked, the clearer the images became.

Kathryn saw fragments of her childhood playing out—her parents laughing, their voices echoing faintly in her mind. She watched the moment the paperwork was signed, sealing her adoption by her aunt and uncle after her parents died in a car accident.

Scattered across the black veils were both moving and still images, haphazardly strewn snapshots of her courtship with Alex, moments both fleeting and profound.

Then, she saw the birth of her daughter—but not through her own eyes. She realized she was seeing it through Alex's. She could feel his emotions and his unwavering strength. The steel resolve in his soul, the silent promise that he would sacrifice everything to keep his family safe and happy.

"I am so sorry I ever doubted you." She said to the image of her husband.

The images darkened to a shade of gray. Kathryn froze in dread as she saw the moment the doctor told them their daughter was slowly dying from something there was no cure for.

The images flickered like pages riffling through a book—countless scenes of doctors, emergency rooms, and anxious nights. Then, the motion stopped. The image held still, showing the moment when she signed the paperwork allowing their daughter to receive palliative care at home.

The multiple screens faded out, melting into the darkness—except for one. It held a memory, slightly out of focus, that Kathryn knew was not one of her own.

The image of showed her daughter with a woman she did not recognize. They spoke of change, opportunity, and choices. Though no sound came from the screen, Kathryn understood every word they were saying.

She watched as her daughter stood, took the woman's hand, and walked toward the screen. The darkening image shimmered, like a stone cast into the center of a calm, black lake.

Then, the woman came into focus. She stepped forward, emerging from the rippled circle onto the lit walkway—just steps away from Kathryn.

The bronzed-skinned, golden-haired woman wore a white dress interwoven with diverse colors. Her dark green eyes were beyond natural.

With a wave of her hand, a single image appeared against the endless black velvet. It was the moment her aunt and uncle told her that her parents had died.

"Is this the reason you cannot let your daughter go?" the woman asked. "Because another family member passed away without saying goodbye to you?"

Kathryn screamed and swung at her. Her hand passed through the woman's incorporeal body, and she stumbled to the edge of the path.

She touched the darkness, and a frigid cold pierced deep into her chest.

The woman seized Kathryn's right arm and pulled her back from the edge.

"Careful. If you had fallen into the darkness, I would not have been able to save you. You would disappear into the nothingness, Kathryn."

"How do you know my name?"

"All who enter this Realm are known to me and the Others who dwell just beyond this Place. Can I suggest we discuss your situation in a less dangerous location?

"And my name is Rain. Now we know each other's names."

With a wave of her hand, the blackness vanished, replaced by the image of a vast forest. The road beneath them transformed into a well-tended dirt path. The gate of light remained, pulsing in sync with Kathryn's heartbeat.

"As you can see, the images may change, but their meaning remains the same in this Place of Making."

"Place of Making? What do you mean by that?"

"This is a place where the spirit and mind are one. Here you can create what you wish to see and decide who you wish to be. The imagination is the only limitation.

"This space exists between two worlds—the Living and the Beyond. The choices made here can be carried into the next Realm of your choosing."

"What do you want from me, Rain?"

"I think you are mistaken. You found yourself here by your own circumstances. So, the question should be: what is it that you want?"

"Answers," Kathryn said. She cupped her hands over her mouth and nose, closing her eyes to steady herself. "Why did you take my daughter from me? Why did you take away my parents?"

Rain's expression remained calm. "I think you misunderstand who and what I am. I didn't take your parents. Nature and timing had a hand in their passing.

"The roads that night were slick with ice. Your father swerved to avoid a deer. The car hit a frozen patch on the bridge. He fought to regain control, but by then, it was too late."

"How did you know what happened if you weren't involved?"

"As I said before, the Others and I are given knowledge of those who enter our Realm. We escort and protect those who travel from the physical world to the next Place.

"We do not cause harm. We relieve them of their pain and fears. Your parents were guided into another Realm of existence by one of the Others. I do not know which One assisted them, but I do know that your parents will be waiting for you in the Realm of Light when your time comes. If you were worried about their fates, you need not be."

Relief washed over Kathryn's face—then vanished just as quickly.

"But what about my daughter? Why did you take her? She was too young to be brought here."

Rain motioned for her to sit.

On the side of the road, a table, two chairs, and a tea set appeared. Kathryn hesitated, then reached out to touch the teapot. It was warm. Rain sat down and poured herself a cup.

"I, myself, prefer tea, but I believe you are a coffee connoisseur?"

From the same teapot, Rain poured a darker liquid.

Kathryn was taken aback but quickly regained composure. A moment ago, she had been in a panic, furious at this woman she believed had destroyed her world. Now, she found herself strangely calm and logical.

She inhaled the aroma of her coffee, the scent transporting her to calmer times—before illness and death had unraveled her family. Kathryn whispered through a thoughtful smile, "Kona from Hawaii."

Not sipping the coffee, she placed the cup back onto the table and exhaled slowly.

"So, can you explain to me why you took my daughter?"

"Your daughter was taken long before I appeared in front of her. The sickness that ravaged her body also weighed heavily on her emotions and mind. The pain became unbearable, but she refused to let go. She worried about you and her father—about how you would feel if she left you."

"How would I feel?" Kathryn's voice wavered. "Did you tell her that my heart would feel like it was being ripped out of my chest? That my world would no longer exist if she were no longer in it?"

"I told her the best way I could, without frightening her."

Kathryn paused, scrutinizing Rain from head to toe before narrowing her eyes.

"How do I know you're not some sort of demon in disguise? That you didn't take my child to your Place to torture her?"

Rain looked over the rim of her cup, a small smile playing on her lips. She spoke as she lowered the cup.

"I can show you that I am not a demon. While I have other guises, I prefer this one for now. Would you like proof that I am not, as you put it, something demonic?"

Kathryn hesitated, then nodded.

"Good. I hope this will be proof enough for you."

Rain twisted her right hand through the air.

The surrounding edges of the pulsing gate radiated a rainbow of colors. Red lay at the bottom, followed clockwise by orange, yellow, green, blue, and purple. Each color seemed to possess a life of its own, pulsing to its own excited rhythm.

The light patterns stretched outward, maintaining their uniformity as they expanded across Rain's domain, enveloping the landscape. The table and chairs now rested on a red path of light.

The gate of light grew larger and drifted closer to where the women sat. Within its center, a shadow appeared. At first, to Kathryn, it was nothing more than a dot blocking the light. But as it expanded, the dark shape transformed into the silhouette of a small human.

Kathryn turned to Rain; her expression was filled with suspicion.

"What are you trying to prove? Showing off your power? Who is that?"

Rain said nothing. She lifted her teacup to her lips, closed her eyes, and took a small sip. Setting the cup back onto the saucer, she interlocked her fingers and rested her chin atop her thumbs.

"You ask who that is," she said at last. "She is the one who gave me my present name. She was the center of your universe. Look deeper into the light, Kathryn. See the child for who she is, not for what she was."

Kathryn turned back toward the light. Her eyes widened in disbelief.

"It couldn't be."

Tears streamed down Kathryn's cheeks. She shot to her feet, nearly knocking over the table, and rushed toward the figure, her pace quickening with every step.

The young girl ran toward Kathryn, leapt into her arms, and wrapped her small arms tightly around her mother's neck.

Kathryn pulled her daughter in as tightly as she could, terrified that if she loosened her grip, the dream would shatter, and her little girl would vanish.

The name of her child formed on her lips. Sniffling back tears, her voice trembling with joy, she whispered.

"Emily."

~*~

Kathryn relaxed her hold on Emily and gently placed her down onto the red path of light. She wiped the hair and tears from her eyes before looking Emily over from head to toe, comparing how she once looked to how she appeared now.

Her once matted, thin blonde hair now cascaded in soft curls and waves. The pain and exhaustion that once clouded her eyes had vanished, replaced by joy and relief. Her skin, once gray with visible veins just beneath the surface, now glowed with a healthy pink hue.

The dress she wore shimmered like woven gold, falling just below her knees, with a silver ribbon tied at the back of her waist. White knee-high socks covered her legs, and delicate silver slippers adorned her feet.

Everything about Emily reminded Kathryn of Rain—even the way she stood, radiating a presence larger than life.

"Mother," Emily said, "what are you doing here?"

"I missed you so much. I wanted to be with you, but you left me. My heart couldn't take it. But you're here now. I get to be with you now."

"I love seeing you, Mom, but it's not your time to be here."

"What do you mean? Of course I'm supposed to be here."

"What I mean is that you don't belong here yet."

Emily took a few steps forward, putting distance between herself and her mother. Turning toward Rain, she demanded, "What is my mother doing here? You promised me she would understand. You lied to me."

Rain rose from her seat, facing Emily.

"I am sorry. My intention was to relieve you of your pain. I did tell you the truth—I said your mother would be sad, but her grief ran deeper and darker than most. I regret not telling you that this might be a possibility.

"But you are right. She does not belong here. Her body and mind will call her back soon."

A wave of panic-struck Kathryn. The thought of losing her daughter again was unbearable.

"No! I'm not losing her again!"

In a desperate lapse of reason, she snatched up Emily and bolted toward the direction her daughter had come from. Emily's voice rang in her ears. "Mom, stop!"

Kathryn didn't listen.

As she approached the gate of light, she squeezed her eyes shut and ran straight into it.

~*~

After taking ten steps through the gate, Kathryn opened her eyes—only to have all thoughts of escape drain from her as she gazed upon Rain.

Rain sat at the table, calmly sipping her tea in an endless forest.

"I am sorry. You cannot leave here without my permission, and Emily is unable to leave with you," Rain said.

"I want my daughter to come back with me. Dammit, let me have her!"

"We both know she would return with you if she could. But here is the truth, she is now a spirit. She no longer has a physical form in the real world.

"If she did, would you really want to trap her back in that body especially after seeing her as she is now?

"I brought Emily here so you could see that she is well. If you do not believe she is happy, ask her yourself."

Kathryn looked down at the child draped in gold and silver.

"Are you happy here?"

Emily beamed. "Yes, I am. I get to run, laugh, and play with the other children. I have friends here.

"If you're worried that you'll never see me again, don't be. When your real time comes, I will be here waiting. I will look exactly like this for you—I will not age, and I will wear this outfit.

"If Dad comes before you do, you'll meet us both.

"How is Dad?"

"I have ignored him since the day you left. I was so worried about you, I didn't think about your father—about how he was or how he felt. I've been ugly and mean to him, and that will be something I need to fix."

Emily nodded. "I know he felt bad when I left. If you leave him now too, he might come here the same way you did. Go back and be with him. He needs you. He loves you, and you love him. Maybe once things are better, you and Daddy can have a brother or sister for me."

Kathryn laughed. "That's all you ever talked about. Even now, you still want one."

She closed her eyes, took a deep breath, and exhaled slowly. Then, kneeling down, she kissed Emily all over her cheeks, making the little girl giggle and squirm. Holding her daughter tightly, Kathryn looked up at Rain.

"Okay, Rain, I am satisfied. I'm ready to go back now and I hope that I don't meet you again for many years to come. Please. Take care of her."

Rain gave a gentle nod. "When you return, you will not see me. But Emily will be waiting for you here in the Place of Making."

Kathryn stood and stepped forward, wrapping her arms around Rain in a warm embrace.

"Goodbye and thank you. This has been a gift to me."

She pulled away from Rain, turned, and walked away from the table, closing her eyes. She felt her spirit slipping back into her body, grounding her once more.

Just before she faded completely, she spoke one last time. "Do you want to know something, Rain? You look better than you have been described by some."

With that, her spirit was gone. But in the distance, she could still hear Emily and Rain talking.

"Rain?"

"Yes?"

"What other way are you supposed to look?"

~*~

Kathryn opened her eyes to find herself sprawled on the floor, looking up at Alex and two EMTs.

"Keep calm," Alex said gently. "They think you may have had a heart attack, but your vitals started to level off about two or three minutes ago. How are you feeling, my love?"

She felt his hand intertwined with hers and gave it a gentle squeeze.

"I feel... like the nightmare is over."

Chapter Six - Matt

Rain gazed over the images flickering against the black velvet sky of her realm. Scenes of children from around the world played out before her. She watched as each child's time came and went.

One image caught her attention—a little boy playing cops and robbers in his parents' bedroom. He wore a toy badge on his right side, a plastic holster strapped around his waist, handcuffs dangling from his left wrist. In his right hand, he held his father's gun. The boy leaped around, the weapon swinging loosely in his grip. On one of his hops, the gun slipped from his hands, hit the ground, and fired.

Rain watched as his mother rushed into the room, her face contorted in horror. She cradled her son's lifeless body, her cries for help piercing the silence. Then, the screen went black.

"He will need someone to greet him when he arrives—until his parents come to collect him." Rain's voice was steady, though tinged with sorrow. "Charles, go and greet him."

A dark-haired boy nodded in acknowledgment. Rain kissed him gently on the forehead and sent him on his way.

Turning her attention to another screen, she saw a red-headed teenage girl walking alone through the streets of downtown Seattle. She wore faded blue jeans and a buttoned-down flannel shirt; her arms wrapped around herself. Fear flickered in her eyes as she turned at every sound, every unfamiliar movement.

When the screen turned black, Rain looked away, deep in thought.

She summoned a girl named Rachel. She was in her mid-teens, shorter than Rain, with black hair streaked with blue. A black leather jacket hung over her slender frame.

"Rachel, you understand what she is feeling and what she has been through. Could you go and help her, please? I would have liked to welcome her personally, but there is someone else I need to attend to. I will be here when you and she arrive."

Rachel nodded. "I'll make her feel safe now that he can't hurt her anymore."

She hugged Rain, accepted a kiss on her forehead, and departed to find the one who needed her help.

~*~

Rain lifted her gaze to the next image. A ten-year-old boy sat quietly in a chair in his bedroom, staring at the closed door. His room was filled with images of superheroes—tattered posters covered the walls, their edges curled and worn. A faded Hulk blanket lay crumpled on the bed. Ragged comic books were strewn across the floor.

Rain turned away. She knew what was going to happen next.

Rising from her chair, she swept her hand through the air, and the images dissipated into the void. She walked over, embraced the children nearby, and set off down the path toward the fields of tall grass.

~*~

Matt waited for his mother to come to his room and punish him for making noise—again.

He had told his friends to be quiet because his mother was sleeping on the couch. He wanted to impress them by showing off the comics he had found, but they had to keep their voices down. His friends tried, but one of them reached for a comic and accidentally knocked the table lamp to the floor.

The crash echoed through the trailer. Matt heard his mother stir, then bolt upright, her voice already rising in a scream.

Panic shot through him.

"You have to go," he whispered urgently, shoving his friends toward the side door. They didn't argue. One by one, they hurried out, disappearing into the night.

Matt turned back, bracing himself.

Matt returned to his room, closed the door behind him, and sat down, resting his hands in his lap as he waited for his mother.

In the kitchen, he heard glass bottles clinking together, the sound sharp and careless. The cupboard doors banged open and shut as if she were searching for something.

"Goddamn kid can't keep quiet while I sleep. I gotta work tonight."

Matt's mother left the trailer at four in the afternoon and didn't return until eight the next morning. He had to fend for himself, making do with whatever food was in the house—when there was any at all.

~*~

Every night, after she was gone, he returned to his room and spent hours flipping through his comics, committing them to memory.

He had found the comics in a pile of discarded boxes near a recycling bin on the side of the road. Water damage had left the pages tough, torn, and gray, their colors faded with time. But they were his. He carefully tacked the damaged posters to his walls and spread the

Hulk blanket pulled from a heap of wet, discarded trash across his bed. It made him feel safe.

~*~

Now, he listened as his mother's footsteps moved down the hall toward his doorway. Every few steps, her palm slapped against the wall for balance. He could hear the slosh of liquid inside the glass bottle she carried.

She would return home with different bottles—and different people. Sometimes men, sometimes women. They would disappear into her room, the door slamming shut behind them.

After her company had left, she would emerge, weary and disheveled, and collapse onto the couch, falling asleep with the television still on.

~*~

She smashed her fist on the door of Matt's room. He got up and headed for the door. As he reached it, he heard what sounded like a thunderclap coming from the door itself.

There were multiple bangs on the door, and it bent in three places.

She walked in, slamming the door open, and glared at Matt. Her shoulder-length brown hair was heavy with dirt and oil. She wore a flannel bathrobe, parts of which were torn. The pocket on the lower left side dangled by the bottom stitches. The strap was tied loosely in front, revealing pieces of her bra and panties.

In her left hand, she held a bottle. Matt could read the word Jack on it.

But the item in her right hand frightened him most of all.

The black leather belt.

That belt had left more than a few bruises in the past, resulting in awkward conversations at Matt's school about clumsy accidents.

Once, he couldn't sit at the dinner table for days because of one of her whippings. Then, his mother forgot why and became upset when he refused to sit, punishing him again.

"What did I tell you? Well? I'm sure I told you not to make any noise. But did you listen to me? No, you didn't. You had to go ahead and do what you wanted and ignore what I told you."

He tried to say I'm sorry, but the belt lashed across the right side of his face, a burning slash.

"Don't you dare say another goddamn word. I'm over your excuses."

She swung the belt again, this time striking the other side of his face.

Matt fell to his knees, crying from pain and fear.

"Don't try that shit with me, mister. I didn't hurt you that bad," she said, lifting his chin with the underside of her hand. "Do you know how long it's going to take me to go back to fucking sleep? Now, tell me you're sorry for waking me up."

"I tried to—"

The belt seared across his face again.

"I didn't say give me an excuse. I said, tell me you're sorry that you woke me. Don't try to say, 'but Mom' or 'let me tell you.' All I want to hear from your mouth is 'I'm sorry.' Got it? 'I'm sorry.' Now, say it."

"I'm sorry."

"Good. Now, I want you to stay in your room while I try to go back to sleep. And don't you dare make another fucking noise. Don't you dare say another goddamn word."

She turned to leave when she heard her son mutter something under his breath.

"WHAT DID YOU SAY?"

Startled, he looked up. "Nothing! Mom!"

"Repeat what you just said. Now!"

He hesitated for a second. "I wish Dad was here."

She stormed at her son, rage in her eyes. She reached out Matt and slammed the bottle against the top and side of his head. The bottle shattered on impact. The exploding glass and its contents sprayed across the walls of his bedroom. His posters were left covered in cuts and whiskey.

"Don't you ever say that again! It was your fault that he left in the first place. He was a horrible excuse for a man. If you think that piece of shit is going to come and get you, you can forget about it. He cares even fucking less for you than I do. At least I feed you. He's so strung out you'd be lucky if he even knows you exist."

His mother's words were garbled, her voice fading as his body slumped to the floor. He heard a dull roar in his ears after the bottle crashed into him. The place where it struck burned with a prickling heat, spreading with every heartbeat.

Matt's thoughts drifted, wondering why his mother hated him. All he could see was the hurt she had caused.

The words "my fault, it's all my fault" formed in his mind. His heartbeat sped up, and his breathing turned shallow.

He lay there as she went back to the kitchen to grab another bottle. Matt tried to cry out for help but couldn't remember who that person in the other room was—the one slamming cabinet doors, making all that noise.

The last words that came from him were, "Please, don't be mad at me. I promise I'll be quiet."

The room tilted, then went black.

~*~

He awoke from the blackness and looked around his room. Something was there that he didn't like—the images of his supposed heroes.

He believed they would protect him from his mother. Superheroes could save the world from monsters, aliens, mad scientists, and common crooks, but they couldn't protect him when she became angry.

He ran through his room, tearing the images from the walls. He took a pair of scissors and slashed at a picture of his father; one he had taken from his mother's room years ago.

His father hadn't helped him. He had abandoned him. He had left him alone in that place.

With her.

Matt sat down on the carpet, pulled a pile of comic books toward him, and started ripping them apart.

"What are you doing?" came a girl's voice from behind him.

He turned his head and saw a young Black girl standing in his room. She wore a white knee-high dress and slippers with silver buckles on top. Her thick, black, curly hair was long enough to be pulled back into a bun. She tilted her head, bobbing it around to see over Matt's shoulders.

Not recognizing her, he asked, "What are you doing here?"

"Looking," she said matter-of-factly. "So, what are you doing?"

"Ripping up my comics."

"Why?"

"They didn't help when I needed them to."

"Oh." She sat down beside him. "What were they supposed to do?"

He put down the comic in his hand. "The people in these go out and help those in need."

"But they are on paper. How can they help in real life?"

"They're supposed to give courage to the reader and make them feel like they aren't alone because they also have issues to solve—to make their world a better place."

"Are they able to do that in the books?"

"Sometimes." He took a breath. "Most of the time, no. But they keep trying. They keep picking themselves up from the ground and trying again, knowing they could fail again."

"I like that way of thinking," she said.

"What's your name? I don't recognize you, but you seem familiar."

"Abbie sent me. My name is Rain. I have been called by different names. Some of the names I have been called are not so nice. One of my friends called me Rain, and it has stayed with me ever since."

"Like Storm," Matt said.

Rain gave him a questioning look.

Matt looked down and started shuffling through the comics. He grabbed an issue with a giant X on the cover, opened it, found an image, and pointed at it.

"This is Ororo. She's from a desert area in Africa. She can control the winds, clouds, and rain. Her friends nicknamed her Storm."

"I like that. A Black female superhero." She pointed at the blanket. "Who is that?"

"Oh. That's the Hulk. His real name is Bruce. He was abused as a child by an alcoholic father. Bruce suppressed his own personal anger and turned it towards his studies."

"Then why is he green?"

"Because of an accident. After it happened, whenever he couldn't control his emotions, he'd lash out at those who did him wrong."

She looked around. "That is kind of what you did in this room, right?"

"Yeah." He nodded. "It seems strange that you don't know some of these characters."

"I am more of a book reader. Have you read Great Expectations or The Strange Case of Dr. Jekyll and Mr. Hyde? The Hulk reminds me a little bit of them."

"No, but I think the second book is what Hulk was based on."

"Who is that?" Rain asked, pointing to another comic.

"Peter or Bruce? Both of their histories are the same and different. They both lost their parents tragically when they were young…"

~*~

Matt and Rain talked about the comics in front of them and the books they had read.

"Rain?" he said while slowly paging through the graphic novel The Crow by James O'Barr.

"Yes?" she replied, watching as the pages rifled past, the images of the story unfolding before her.

"My mother went too far this time, didn't she?" His voice was neutral.

She stopped looking down and lifted her head toward him. She dropped all childlike fascinations on her face. Her voice changed to an adult understanding of the question.

"Yes."

He closed the graphic novel. "And there's nothing I can do to change what happened, is there?"

"No."

"Why did she do what she did? Why is she that way?"

"For some," Rain explained, "they are not wired right from the beginning. They lash out at others because they do not understand themselves.

"Others fall victim to something called generational abuse. The anger and pain from their past were layered onto them by those who likely suffered the same abuses.

"They try to bury their overwhelming past hurts by distracting themselves instead of confronting the issues head-on. This continues until someone breaks the unhealthy cycle and learns from the past mistakes of others. You might have been the one to change your family's story."

Rain paused and took a breath. "Unfortunately, it was your mother who broke the cycle. And for that, I am sorry for you."

Matt exhaled. "This is why I haven't been afraid of her coming into my room for some time now. That's why you're here, isn't it? To tell me something I just figured out."

"I am here to do what we have been doing. I got to spend a little time talking about books, comics, and other stories with you. I wanted to keep you happy and relaxed before either you figured it out or when it was time for me to tell you."

"That I died?" he said.

"No. That you are beyond her ever hurting you again."

Matt thought about what had happened to him and asked, "This isn't the first time you've sat down with someone like me, is it?"

"No, it is not. There have been others like you. I have listened to them talk about their love of books, television, sports, and movies. They needed something to let their mind escape the reality life had given them. They wanted to talk to someone who would listen— someone who cared about what they were passionate about. They just wanted to feel important, to feel like they mattered to someone, even for a little while."

Rain smiled. "Now, you brought up Storm. Thank you for that. I have always been partial to her. As powerful as she is, she always has to keep her emotions in check, or something could go wrong. I understand her personality and restraint. If I let go of my own emotions, I could affect everything around me. I try my best not to fail at my responsibility to help who I can when it matters most."

Matt smiled.

"I do have a real superpower. Are you interested in seeing it?"

Matt's eyes widened. "What is it?"

"I am a shapeshifter."

"Really? Can I see it? How's it done?"

"I place an image in my mind of how I want to look and build it up around me. In most cases, I take the form of a grown woman of wonderment."

Rain stood up from the ground and dusted off her dress as if smoothing out the wrinkles. With every swipe of her hands, her white dress lengthened to her ankles, shimmering with swirling colors. The slippers on her feet faded away, leaving her barefoot on the floor.

Matt watched as she transformed before his eyes. She grew taller, her frame becoming more muscular. Her skin deepened to a rich bronze, and her hair loosened from its bun, lengthening into long wavy golden-brown strands.

"What do you think?" Rain asked.

"Wow. I like it, but the color of your skin and hair is very unusual."

"The colors I use are a blend of different races because I want to represent as many as I can. To me, no one is above another. We are all one."

"So, what do we do now? What happens to me?" Matt asked.

"You are in a special situation that we must consider. Ultimately, it depends on you. Once we walk out of this room and leave your place, some decisions will have to be made."

"I have choices?"

"Many. One is staying in the Place that I watch over. It is filled with nature, children, and activities. You would have your fill of endless joys. You would meet others like yourself, looking for friendship and someone to talk to and play with. But..."

"But?"

"But when the others that come are here, they are in waiting. When their families come for them..."

"They would be gone, and I'd have to start over with someone new." Matt replied. "I would be in a place with no hope of somebody coming for me."

Rain nodded.

"What else could I do?"

"You could become who you always wanted to be—a superhero."

Matt's face brightened.

"You could change your appearance to become that mysterious figure who goes out into the world to fight the evils of darkness. This Place allows you to transform yourself, through the strength of your mind, heart, and soul. You would be what you always wanted to be—and more—if that is what you desire."

Matt stood up tall, clenched his fists, pressed them against his ribs, and lifted his chin high.

Rain laughed at the familiar stance.

Matt's expression on his face turned serious, and he slowly lowered his hands.

"There are no real villains here to fight, are there?"

Rain lowered her eyes. "No. We left them when we came to this Place."

Rain stepped forward and offered Matt a hug. He accepted, and she placed a small kiss on the crown of his head.

"There could be a lot of choices, but there's not many that would make me happy, right?" he said.

She released him and stepped away. "There is another option for you to consider. Your knowledge and life in the world was limited. Because of your fear of punishment—and not wanting to lose what little love you believed you had with your mother, your life consisted of the house, your school, and this very room we are now looking at.

"Your lack of experiences does not allow you to soar. As I have said, I do have a different option."

"What's that?"

"A mentor. Someone who would escort you to all the wonders you have only heard about. They would be able to teach you about the things and places you missed out on."

"Can you mentor me? It sounds like fun to learn from you and visit all those places."

"If it were that easy, I would consider it," Rain said, smiling. "But outside of this Place, I have my own responsibilities to watch over. And right now, someone else fills the role you suggested for yourself."

"Oh." Matt's response drifted to a whisper.

"I give my word to you that the person you meet with will be exactly what you need, and you will not be disappointed."

"I guess I can try. You wouldn't lie to me, right?"

Rain smiled. "You, little one, are too smart for me to do that to you—even if I could."

Matt nodded in agreement.

Rain closed her eyes and sent a message for help to the Others, then waited for their response.

After a few moments, she tilted her head upward as if listening, then nodded.

"Matt, are you ready to leave this room?"

"Yes."

"Good. He will meet us outside," Rain said, stepping through Matt's bedroom doorway.

He followed closely behind but first peered down the hallway to make sure his mother wasn't there.

Rain reached for the knob, opened the door, and stepped through.

Matt looked through the opening into a sunny afternoon sky. A few steps in front of Rain stood a man who looked like someone his mom would bring home on multiple occasions—except he didn't have a bottle in his hand or a cigarette in his mouth.

The man was taller than Rain. His shoulder length hair and trimmed beard were deep brown. He wore a pair of wire-framed glasses, blue jeans, a white T-shirt, and a black leather jacket. In his hands, he held two helmets—one smaller than the other.

"Hello there. You must be Matt. My name is Logan."

Matt's jaw dropped, recognizing the name.

Logan smiled. "No, not that Logan. He's a bit shorter than I am—with one heck of a temper. I'm also a bit of a comic geek myself."

He reached out his hand with a friendly smile. "It's a real pleasure to meet you."

Matt stepped out of the doorway and down two of the three steps below but kept his distance.

Logan lowered his hand. "I understand and respect that. I was told to come here to meet you and Rain. I hope you and I can become friends."

Rain spoke. "Matt, this is a person I would have the honor of calling my hero. Throughout his life, he helped many children escape from dangerous situations. He rescued them from bad homes and tried to find them safer places to live, where they could hopefully be loved."

"I was raised in a life much like yours," Logan said, "but I survived and went to school so I could help others like us. Over the years, I wanted to save as many as I could. I did save some, but there were so many that I couldn't. Even with all the missed opportunities, I never stopped trying."

"Did you adopt any of them?" Matt asked.

"I wasn't allowed to adopt any of them, as much as I wanted to. There were laws during my life that didn't allow a single man to adopt, most of the time. And there were even harsher laws for those who had same gender partners.

"But I continued helping those I could, making sure they had a brighter future so they wouldn't be trapped in the darkness of their pasts."

"That is why the Others I cooperate with asked Logan to come here," Rain said. "If you would like, Logan and you can travel beyond this Place of Making and explore what you may have only dreamed of."

"Place of Making?" Matt questioned.

"This is a Place where you decide what you want to do and where you want to go. Sometimes, the trauma of life traps someone in their own world, hindering them from moving on. My responsibility is to try and save those that I can and, like Logan said, to help give them a brighter future.

"He and I would like to offer you an opportunity to become Logan's ward. He is willing to educate you, answer your questions, and, when the time is right, take you to the next Place of your choosing. He will be an open book and a fountain of knowledge for you. All you have to do is say yes to begin."

Matt threw his arms around Rain and whispered, "Yes." Then he released her and turned to Logan. "I'm ready."

"All right then." Logan handed Matt the smaller helmet. Matt placed it on his head and found that it fit perfectly.

"Matt, could you go to the motorcycle and settle into the sidecar? I need to finish talking to Rain, okay?"

"Okay," Matt said as he moved toward the bike. "What kind of motorcycle is it?"

"A Harley, of course," Logan said as he winked at Rain. "What other motorcycle is there?"

Matt waved to Rain. "Goodbye, Rain. Thank you." He smiled and ran off toward the motorcycle.

"Thank you, Rain," Logan said. "I think this will work out for both of us. I do have a question. What will he remember about his family? I don't want to sound mean, but to him, I may never be his family, and he may never trust me."

"One day, he will see you as his family. Even as we speak, those memories of hate and those who created them are slowly disappearing from Matt's mind. He will be his own person, but he will know you as his parent.

"This also works both ways. The longer you are with him, the more you will believe that he is your son."

"That will make me happy, and I promise you that I will do all I can to make his new life one happily worth remembering," Logan said. "I don't know much about what defines a hero, but I do believe a hero help those they meet and makes them feel happy and safe, no matter what kind of life they may have lived. I'd like to say that I am honored to count you as one of my heroes."

A smile crossed Rain's face. She leaned forward, kissed Logan on the forehead, and said, "Thank you."

Logan nodded to her, walked over to his motorcycle. He swung his leg over the seat, placed his helmet on his head, started the engine, and then drove off with Matt at his side.

"Which way are we going first?" Matt asked.

Logan pointed. "Second star from the left and straight on till morning."

Chapter Seven - Pamela and Rachel

Rain turned her attention to another screen. On it was an image of a red-headed teenage girl wearing faded blue jeans and a buttoned-down flannel shirt. She was walking alone through the streets of downtown Seattle, fearfully turning her head at every sound or movement that was unfamiliar to her.

Past images flickered onto the screen, showing Pamela upset that her parents grounded her for two weeks for staying out too late the night before. She told them that she wasn't doing anything wrong and she just wanted to look at the Seattle city lights from the top of Iron Works Hill, near the sun calendar. But she lost track of time and had to rush home.

They didn't listen to her excuse and sent her to her bedroom for the night.

In a moment of frustration, anger, and teenage impulse rebellion, she ran off.

A passing city bus startled Pamela as she wandered near Pike Street and the Pike Place Market, gazing at and around the closed shops. During the daylight hours, the area would be packed with people hunting for deals and curios. Crowds would gather around in front of the fish market to watch as wild salmon, tuna, and other catches were tossed through the air between vendors, an entertaining spectacle, before the fish were wrapped up for customers to depart with.

Some of the wanderers would pick up random tidbits off the shop shelves or grab samples from the deli counters to help them decide what they wanted to eat for lunch or dinner later. In the lower levels of the marketplace, the bookstores and souvenir shops were always crowded from the moment they opened until closing time.

Seattle's bustling shopping district, now well past midnight, the shops were dark and empty, except for the faint overhead glow of the Pike Place Market sign and a random homeless person. All the shops had metal gates protecting their entrances and valuables from unwanted break-ins.

A cold shiver ran through as Pamela passed by the dark corners and alleys of the now-abandoned Pike, Western, and Union Streets. She wondered why she had been so stubborn—why she had disobeyed her parents' punishment.

"Maybe if I went home now, they would only ground me for a month. I could live with that." She told herself. "Right now, I could live with two months."

She drew in a deep breath and turned toward the direction of the bus that had passed her a few minutes ago.

Her decision to leave came a step too late.

From one of the darkened passages, a pair of hands lunged out, grabbing her around the neck and mouth.

Her eyes widened in fear as she struggled, but the hands dragged her backward into the shadows.

The grip twisted her around before shoving her forcefully onto the ground.

A tall, unkempt white man with a scraggly beard moved around and hovered over her face. His right hand tightened around her neck, and in a gravelly voice, he spoke.

"Quiet now. You wouldn't want to get hurt too badly, wouldja?"

She barely managed to shake her head, signaling that she would stop fighting.

His left hand slid down and grabbed hold of her flannel shirt, yanking it open and ripping the buttons off. He unlatched the front of her bra, exposing her breasts, before moving his hand to her blue jeans. He pulled at the button and zipper until they came undone.

Then, gripping both her jeans and underwear in his fist, he forced them down over her hips and thighs.

He smiled when he saw his prize.

The man lowered himself onto Pamela, pressing his weight against her. She could feel him shifting, forcing her legs apart. With one foot, he pushed down on her jeans, sliding them from her knees to her ankles. He adjusted his position, reached down with his left hand, and pulled at the waistband of his sweatpants. Then, shifting his hips, he slammed himself into her.

Terror and pain exploded through her senses as he ripped into her body. She screamed, crying out, her fingers clawing at the pavement in pain.

She wanted it to stop.

It wouldn't stop!

He didn't stop!

He was tearing her apart!

With each brutal thrust, her insides shrieked from the damage he was inflicting.

"I said not a word."

His right hand gripped her throat so tightly that any sound that tried to escape her mouth as a gurgle. When no air returned to her lungs, she struggled to inhale.

She slapped his arm, repeatedly in a desperate plea for release to her throat.

He moved his left hand behind her head and gripped the nape of her neck.

"Fine then. Don't need you here anyway."

With a hard twist of his hands, she heard the sickening crack of bones in her ears and heard the echo of it reflect off the corridor walls.

Her body contorted once then went still.

Pamela felt the darkness and numbness enveloped her.

Then the pain stopped.

Her thoughts turned to her parents, and how she wished she could be home with them.

~*~

When the screen turned black, Rain looked away, deep in thought.

She summoned a girl named Rachel. She was in her mid-teens, shorter than Rain, with black hair streaked with blue. A black leather jacket hung over her slender frame.

"Rachel, you understand what she is feeling and what she has been through. Could you go and help her, please? I would have liked to welcome her personally, but there is someone else I need to attend to. I will be here when you and she arrive."

Rachel nodded. "I'll make her feel safe now that he can't hurt her anymore."

She hugged Rain, accepted a kiss on her forehead, and departed to find the one who needed her help.

~*~

Pamela awoke, shivering in a corner of cold concrete.

She was still in the place where it happened.

She hadn't seen the man leave. She didn't even know how she had ended up in the corner—only that she was there and didn't want to move away from it.

Her mind continuously replayed what he had done to her.

How many times he had shoved himself into her body?

Over and over.

Harder and harder.

Her screams, trapped inside her, unheard.

Over and over and over, and… "Shhh.

Hush now. It's over…."

The voice sounded like hers.

Female. Young. Soft-spoken and calm.

"It will never be over! It just keeps going on and on and on and…"

She kept repeating on and on for a time before finally falling silent, though the words still echoed inside her mind.

The voice spoke again. "You're right. It's never over. It will always be there."

"How could he do that to me? I'm just a kid. Just a little girl. How could he?"

Her voice was garbled, thick with tears. Her nose ran. She sniffled between breaths.

"He didn't care. To him, you weren't human just something to use and dispose of. They don't ask for forgiveness afterward because they forget. And then they move on to the next."

"I'm so afraid he's coming back for me. For more!"

Pamela shivered, curling into a small ball, her eyes locked on the opening in front of her.

"Calm yourself. He won't return. I promise you."

"Your promises mean nothing! You don't know what he did to me!"

She broke down into sobs.

"I know what he did." The other voice said, that was filled with hurt, echoing through the space.

"He damaged your body. He destroyed your soul, your heart, and your desires. Most of all, he obliterated your dreams.

"I know that he will always be in your nightmares. The dream of that perfect person you will love is now marred by his grotesque face.

"And your dreams for the future? Gone. Taken away from you, forever."

The voice, that was not quite Pamela, trailed into silence.

There was something in her words—an undeniable truth. It carried a pain that Pamela recognized.

For a long moment, neither of them spoke. There was a quiet understanding between them, one that didn't need to be acknowledged.

Pamela was the first to break the silence. "Who are you?"

"My name is Rachel. I'm here to help you. Can I have your name?"

Another pause. Then, in a small voice, "Pamela. My name is Pamela."

"Hello, Pamela. I'm sorry we had to meet this way."

"I want to call my mom and dad. I want them to pick me up." Pamela sobbed. "Please, Rachel? Can you give them a call for me?"

"I don't have a cell phone. I wish I did. It would've helped me out when I needed it."

"Can you go to the pay phone? I saw one earlier. Right out there." She pointed toward the darkened entrance.

"I'm sorry. It's no longer there."

"What are you talking about? I saw it."

"All I can tell you is that it's no longer there. Besides, I don't really want to leave you alone right now."

Pamela thought about being alone again.

"You're right. I don't want to be alone right now."

She looked up from her corner and surveyed the area. It was a delivery bay. She sat between the prep area on her right and a cement stair on her left.

"Pamela, would it be all right if I came closer? Maybe I can help you clean up help you feel a bit warmer."

"He tore my shirt. He ripped my bra. He damaged my jeans. He…"

She broke down, burying her face in her lap.

When she finally regained control of herself, she continued. "I can't put any of it back together."

Rachel spoke. "Please. Allow me to help you."

In a quiet, exhausted voice, Pamela replied, "All right."

"I will take this very slowly. I'm not going to come at you. If you want me to stop, just tell me. I'll understand."

Rachel walked around toward the front of Pamela so she could see her approach.

Pamela listened to the soft clomps of Rachel's boots. The sound of the steps seemed to move further away.

About twenty feet away, Pamela saw Rachel walk down a set of stairs on the right side of the area.

She looked Rachel over as she approached. Her black hair, streaked with blue, was wild yet styled. She wore black jeans, a black leather jacket, a torn blue midriff shirt, and combat boots.

Rachel moved toward Pamela; her hands open to show she held nothing.

"Nothing to hurt you, I promise."

Rachel stopped just in front of Pamela, then lowered herself onto the cement, sitting on her knees with her hands resting on her lap.

"Come on. Let me look at you."

Pamela hesitated before raising her head to face Rachel.

~*~

Rachel saw dirt smudges on Pamela's face and red finger marks on her neck where the man had grabbed her.

She pulled a rag from inside her jacket, dampened it in a small puddle to her right, and brought it to Pamela's face.

Rachel wiped at a few dirt spots as she spoke. "There you go. A bit better, I think. I can almost see you under there." She smiled, trying to lighten the mood and help Pamela relax.

"There's nothing to look into. How bad am I?"

Rachel looked her over. "You look fine, except for the dirt. Why don't you straighten up your jeans, and let's see what we can do about your shirt, okay?"

"Alright."

Pamela pulled her jeans back up over her hips. Her upper thighs were tender, and the fabric made her wince. She paused, steeled herself, and continued pulling them up to her waist. The pain was worst when the jeans pressed against her crotch.

Rachel examined the buttonless shirt. "You need to take off your bra."

Pamela panicked. "What?" She instinctively curled in on herself.

Rachel calmly spoke. "The bra is damaged. It'll just hang there and be uncomfortable for you."

"Oh." She relaxed.

Slipping off her flannel shirt, she crossed an arm over her chest to shield herself from any unseen eyes. She removed the torn bra and put her shirt back on.

"Can I?" Rachel asked, lifting her hands toward the bottom of the shirt.

Pamela gave a silent nod, watching carefully as Rachel took the bottom of the shirt, rolled it up, and evened out the sides. She tied off the rolled edges, securing it snugly around Pamela's waist and chest area.

"That should hold for now. It isn't much, but it should make you feel less exposed."

"Thank you. You seem calm. You're careful and not nervous about what happened to me. Why is that?"

"Because I've also been through what happened to you," Rachel said, her voice hollow and haunted.

Pamela noticed Rachel's eyes were fixated—not on a place in front of her, but on a place in time.

"I've lived it. It was horrible. It filled me with so much hate that dug deep into my soul."

Pamela considered Rachel's confession for a moment. Then, gently, she cupped Rachel's hand with her own.

"What happened to you?"

Rachel blinked, breaking out of her trance. She looked down, noticing Pamela's hands touching hers. Then she lifted her gaze back to Pamela.

Taking a deep breath, Rachel stared off into the nothingness and spoke, her voice soft and slow.

~*~

I was going on a date, my very first date. The first one my parents had allowed me to go on. It was two weeks after my birthday, and I was massively excited.

My date was with a high school senior named Ken, a blond-haired, well-built boy, who played in multiple high school sports. I've seen him during my time at school before but always felt like I was below his radar.

I was a sophomore, and I dressed a lot like this. I loved my look because it made me feel confident and strong. Most kids at school ignored me, of course, because I stood out.

One morning before first-period class, he walked right up to me and asked me out. I was completely shocked. I said yes immediately.

That still bothers me, even now, because I never questioned his intentions or my response. I just took it for what it was worth.

He smiled and returned to his friends.

Two nights later I was standing in front of my bathroom mirror, drying my hair, applying my makeup, and putting on my favorite dress that I had picked out for a moment like that.

Since the dress was blueberry colored, I made sure my lipstick, eyeshadow, and purse matched. I'd been waiting so long for my parents to allow me to go on a date that I had bought my whole outfit earlier in the year.

I was psyched and ready to go. I looked over myself one last time, added a large black belt around my waist for my personal style, and went downstairs to wait for Ken.

I waited for more than a half an hour past the time of my date looking out my kitchen window and felt like I was being stood up. My parents sat in the living room, checking in on me from time to time. I knew they were disappointed for me. I loved them for that. Not for the check-ins, but for the concerns that were in their eyes.

I finally got tired of waiting around. I was pissed and headed back upstairs to take off my makeup and dress off. It was then that there was a knock at the door. I saw the top of combed blonde hair through the door's window. It had to be him.

I ran back down the stairs and almost missed the last three steps. I beat my dad to the door by less than two steps. I kissed him on the cheek, smiled, and said, "I love you, Dad. Be home by midnight, okay?" I slipped out the door before he could answer.

Ken was wearing a casual but dressy black suit, a light gray shirt, and a red tie. He looked good. Really good. And as we approached his car, I noticed that the color of his tie matched the car.

"You look nice, Rachel," he said to me.

"Thank you. So do you, but your car is hot."

He smiled. "A pre-graduation present from my parents."

"Nice gift. All my family can afford is putting me through my first year of college. And I still have another two years before I graduate."

"I got a track scholarship, so I get to go to college, but I don't know where I'm going yet. Maybe A&M. Maybe not. So, are you ready to head out?"

"Yep."

As we neared the red Mustang, Ken said, "Sorry I'm late. I had a little trouble finding your house."

I smiled. "As long as it wasn't anything serious, I forgive you. I thought you stood me up."

His smile was charming and warm. "The thought never crossed my mind, and if it did, be kicking myself right now. You look absolutely beautiful more than I could've imagined."

I blushed, my face turning red. I lowered my eyes demurely. A little flirting, I thought, never hurts.

He walked a pace or two ahead of me, reached the passenger side door, and opened it. "Your chariot awaits, dear princess."

Again, I blushed at his comment. I down sat in the car and said, "Thank you, kind sir."

He walked around the back of the car and got inside, rolled down the windows and drove off. It was a warm night, and the wind passing through the open car's window during the drive felt great.

We drove around the areas of Turtle Creek and Oak Lawn for a while, enjoying the music that played on his dashboard's CD player. Somewhere during that time, his hand slipped over to my side and grabbed mine.

"Are you hungry?" he asked. "There's a great Italian restaurant on Northwest Highway and the Tollway, and maybe after that, we might want to go over to Grapevine for a bit."

I checked the time on my watch. It was nearly Seven. "Sure, why not."

He turned the car around and drove toward the restaurant. He lifted my hand and lightly kissed the back of it before lowering it again with a smile. "Thank you for coming with me. I thought for sure you were going to turn me down. I'm glad you didn't. Some of my friends heard that you were fun to be with."

"Give me music and a convertible, and I'm in heaven."

"Then I'm glad you have both. A pretty lady is all I needed to make it a great evening."

We pulled into the parking lot of the restaurant. He got out, walked around, and opened my door for me to get out. He offered his arm for support as I stepped out of the car, and we headed inside.

We were seated at a small table in a corner. We ordered and spent the time waiting for the food just staring at each other. We played footsies and held hands. It was incredible. My heart pounded, and my breathing went shallow.

When the food came, we tried each other's food and went back to staring at each other. By the time we actually started eating, the food was cold. It didn't matter to us; we still ate it.

We stayed at the table for about an hour and a half. Ken paid the bill and escorted me out the door with his arm around the small of my back. A wave of heat climbed up my spine. I leaned my head on the side of his chest.

We slipped back into the car. From there, things started to getting closer between the two of us.

It started with a kiss—warm and passionate. It was everything I dreamt it would be.

He touched my face as he kissed my lips. His hand wandered to my shoulders, caressing them. Then his hand started to slide down. It was at that point, I began to feel a little uncomfortable. I was about to say something when a set of headlights passed through the windshield, distracting us. We pulled apart, he started the car, and we drove out of the parking lot.

"Do you want to go to a friend's party before I take you home?"

"I thought we were going to Grapevine to check out the arcade or see what movies were playing there?"

"We were. I mean, we can, of course. I just want to stop in to say hello. It's on the way there, I promise."

Through nagging self-doubts and mental warnings, one word slipped from my lips. "Alright."

~*~

Rachel focused on Pamela. "On the way there, all we did was hold hands and laugh. In that moment, I truly did have fun being in that car."

"When did the laughs stop?" Pamela asked.

"It was when we entered his friend's home."

~*~

I stood at the doorway of Ken's friend Trip's house, which his father owned. He could've been a twin of Ken, except for his jet-black hair. I always thought he was kind of a jerk. I was told he got his name because he couldn't jump hurdles. He was fast on the dash, but when it came to hurdles, he never could clear them.

I could see through the door and windows that several students from school were inside. The music pouring out sounded like a combination of Linkin Park and Eminem. Basically, the music was slammin'.

When Ken entered the house, it would be the last time I fully saw him for a while. He was like a lion in a tall golden African field.

He blended and disappeared.

He knew the grounds he stalked. I, on the other hand, felt like a peacock stepping into that same field.

I stood out.

Through the moving waves of cloth and flesh, I spotted Ken heading into the kitchen, grabbing a drink from a keg, and then, vanish. Five minutes later, he went past the stairwell banister, looked my way, smiled, and blended back into the field.

This continued for nearly an hour. Meanwhile, others passed me by, giggling a bit, saying how lucky I was to be with Ken, how interesting my choice of colors were, and wondering who the hell I was. I smiled at some those comments because I usually sat next to them in at least one class or another.

There were certain unconscious thoughts that crossed my mind and emotions I didn't recognize that night. I wouldn't be fully aware of them until the end.

A big, bright bird in a field of gold.

Tired of being ignored, I stepped outside for air, debating whether to leave on my own. I looked at the cars parked in front of me. More than half of them cost more than my father's yearly salary.

I didn't belong there, and I really decided that I did not want to belong there.

As I stepped toward the road to get my bearings and try to figure out a way home. I reached for my cell phone inside my purse and heard a crashing sound at the door that made me turn back toward the house.

There was Ken. He stumbled out the door, tripping over his own two feet, trying to run toward me.

"Been looking all over for you. Where have you been hiding?"

I was shocked. He was accusing me of disappearing.

"You dumb son of a—"

"Joke, Blue. Joke." He feathered his hair back from his eyes and stood up straight. "I'm sorry I left you there, dear princess, but I got a bit caught up inside. I didn't mean to ignore you. I saw you walk out the door, and I knew I fucked up."

"Damn straight. Tempted to leave your sorry ass here and start walking home. Can't be more than…"

"Twelve miles, in that direction." He pointed to his right. "Directions get a little muddled around here. Been turned around a few times myself. Once, I found myself in Arlington, by the ball field, before I got my bearings."

"Really? Then what happened?"

"Parked my car, went to the stadium, and watched the game. Figured since I was there, I might as well not let a good thing go to waste." He paused. "Once again, I came out here when I lost you inside and decided that I should not to let a good thing go to waste."

Whatever pissed-off attitude I had was gone in that moment. He leaned in and kissed me lightly.

"Do you want me to take you home?"

"Not quite yet. I'd like to drive around a bit longer in your car and listen to some more music."

~*~

"That was the last real moment of happiness that night," Rachel said. Her hands were cupped lightly around her nose and mouth. Pamela watched as Rachel closed her eyes, took a long breath, and held it for what seemed like a long moment before slowly released into the air.

Rachel steeled herself for what lay ahead in the story. She turned toward Pamela, lowered her hands, and smiled slightly. She was ready to talk once more.

~*~

As we drove in lighted streets of the night, I slowly relaxed into the rhythm of the music on the car stereo and the hum of the road. I forgot time, and I forgot space for a while.

When I looked down at my watch and noticed it was nearing midnight. I glanced around and didn't quite recognize where I was. I knew I had been there before, but I just didn't know where there was.

"Ken, where are we?"

"Heading back into town. There's a shortcut coming up. Don't worry about it. I got control of the situation," he said with that smile that made my knees shake and my heart jump.

We exited off 183 onto Irving Boulevard, heading toward the industrial area of town. I looked over at him, about to question his choice, when he said, "Don't worry, I got this. This is going to save us time."

We continued down the Boulevard and took a quick right to another road. It twisted in shadows as the streetlights drifted away from behind us. Ken increased the speed of his car to take the corners more sharply.

"Aren't we going a little fast?"

There was no answer.

"Ken?"

"Shhh. I'm watching the road."

He took a quick left as the road curved to the right. We followed it until it turned left again. We passed under a bridge and continued. "Aren't we supposed to be up there?"

"No." That was all he said.

We passed by a sign quickly. I caught the words Trinity View Park. It confused me why we were there and why Ken had suddenly gone so silent. My right hand slowly moved toward my purse sitting on my left side. My fingers shifted through the contents, searching for my flip phone.

I couldn't find it in there.

I tried again.

It had to be there.

It wasn't.

I realized I had left it on my bathroom countertop. In my rush to grab everything I needed for my purse; I'd forgotten the one item that would've made all the difference in my life.

The car twisted right, then left, and then just stopped.

I slowed my breathing, even though my heart was about to pulse out of my neck. I turned to him and asked, "Why did we stop here?"

"Sorry. I got turned around for a moment. I'm trying to get my bearings."

"There are two roads here," I said, "one is bound to get us back the right way. Check your phone. Surely you have a GPS system on your phone, right?"

"Don't have the new upgraded phone yet."

"Then let's pick a road and head that way," I said, trying not to sound irritated or scared. I failed at both.

Ken turned toward me and said, "Let's stop here for a few minutes." He shifted the car into Park, removed the keys from the ignition, swung open his door, and stepped out.

"Where are you going?"

"Just stretching my legs." He walked to the front of his car and around to my side. He placed both of his hands on the door and leaned toward me. "Come out of the car and stretch your legs too."

"I'm good here."

"I thought you wanted to kiss a little longer," Ken said. "Better to kiss standing up in my arms than sitting down there." He brushed his hand lightly against my hair.

"I'm no longer in the mood to do that."

"Well then, at least get out of the car for a bit."

"No. Why is it so important that I get out of the car?"

He flashed me a quick, jerked smile and pulled his hands off the car door. "There's no real reason. I just wanted to get a look at you one last time, in that dress, before we get back to your house."

"You can get another look at me when I leave you and your car at MY house."

His hands gripped the door again, and he shook the car violently. "Get out, get out, get out!"

It was then I realized I would be in more danger sitting in a convertible than standing outside of it. I moved my left hand and unfastened the seatbelt. I looked up at him to tell him to move away from the door.

The peacock heads into an open field, where the lion waits.

I stepped out of the car as he moved away from the door. I slowly moved around, shifting ever so slightly to the rear of the car.

"You see, Blue? I told you it's better to get out of the car for a minute." His image from the headlights gave me a chilling feeling in my gut. His perfect blonde quaff was now a little ragged. His eyes were wide open but looked like they saw nothing but me.

There was something else there. At the time, I didn't know what it was, but now I do. It was hunger. Pure and territorial.

The lion locks his sight onto his prey, and the eyes never waver.

His red tie was pulled away from his neck. It was probably interfering with his breathing. He moved toward the backside of the car and me. He closed the door when he reached it.

"You alright, Blue? Didn't mean to give you a scare. I just wasn't ready to head back yet. I just wanted to spend a little more time with you." His eyes scanned me up and down quickly. He brought his right hand forward. "Come here." He tried to sound charming. I shook my head.

"Come. Here." Those two words were more command than request.

The need to flee nearly overran my mind. I had no idea where I was or where to go, but my instincts just told me to run. Into the night, away from this.

I stepped forward to him, looking for any escape from what I feared was coming. I didn't want to see him angered. I raised my right hand to meet his.

"Do you know where we are?" he asked me, with a slight tilt of his neck and a small smile on his lips.

I shook my head.

"I used to play little league baseball here." He said, as my heart dropped in my chest. "I was an outfielder. I could run down almost anything that came my way. Some of them made it over the fence. So, after the games, I used to go out into the back field and collect the balls. After a while, I started to find them easily. From how far they went over the fence and what part of the field they landed in. I always loved coming here." He paused for a moment and then said a voice that haunts me even now. "Still do. Every chance I get."

His left hand grabbed my elbow, and he pulled me toward him. "Now I want a kiss from you. For starters." The grin he gave didn't make me weak at the knees; it gave me a knife-twisting feeling in the gut.

He pushed his body against mine, and I stepped backward. My backside pressed against the car, and I realized I was trapped.

My head dodged in all directions to avoid his hot breath on my face.

His eyes showed anger at my disobedience. He brought the back of his hand across my left cheek. I felt the heat and tasted iron as my eyes watered up.

My face was squeezed between his fingers and his thumb. He yanked my face toward him. I was eye-to-eye with the predator. Whatever I saw before was gone. Any chance of talking my way out of this was now gone.

So was Ken.

I took one last chance to make my escape and struck him where a man is at their most vulnerable.

As my knee slammed into his nuts, he shoved me back and to my left, so he could comfort his area. The side of my head struck the top of the passenger door, scraping my barrette off. I fell off balance and went toward the ground. When my right hand hit the gravel and the palm pressed into the ground, I used the momentum to push off toward the open field.

I don't know when I lost my shoes, but I could feel my feet pressing against the ground to gain extra power. I didn't think of a direction. I just knew I had to keep going because he was back there. Somewhere.

There was an opening in between the high weeds, and I ran in that direction. The light from the park was dissipating as I continued. I just needed a place to hide until morning, when I could see, and maybe he would give up the hunt by then.

I turned right, ran straight, and turned left when the bramble wouldn't let me pass. I ran a little further and saw a dark patch, took a breath, and jumped into it.

Once inside, I held my breath as long as I could and prayed that I was well hidden. I wanted to cry, to scream out, and completely break down into tears. I knew he would find me if I did.

I could hear leaves crunching, branches cracking, grass being sifted through, and him jumping around in them, looking for me. Every noise made me shake uncontrollably.

The lion agitates the bush to startle his prey out of hiding.

"This game is over," he said in a slow, slick, playful cadence. "Time for you to come out now. You know I will find you soon, and when I do, I will make you pay. Oh yes, I will. C'mon. Let's end all this, shall we?"

The son of a bitch was enjoying it.

I heard him hop around in the tall grass a few more times before all the sounds he made stopped, and he no longer made a sound.

I could hear the wind, the stream, and the traffic in the distance, but I could not hear him.

The lion becomes silent.

I've read that just before it happens, lions can move through the brush with such finesse that not a single blade of grass will bend or break. They can get within inches of their prey, and the target wouldn't even know it.

And with that…

His eyes and a large grin appeared in front of me.

"Gotcha!"

The lion pounces on his prey.

And then, everything went black.

~*~

I woke up with my head throbbing and my throat so sore I could barely breathe. I felt confused and forgot where I was for a moment. I tried to remember. There was swinging and fighting. I was fighting so hard, like I was struggling against something or someone.

I sat up, looked around, and couldn't recognize where I was. I didn't know why I was there, but I thought I was here with someone.

"Hello?" I called out. No answer. I called out again. Same response. I was ready to call again when I saw a man walking away from my area toward my right. In his arms, he was carrying something, but I did not see what it was.

I stepped toward him and noticed I got there very quickly. I stood and watched him pass right by me. His blonde hair was disheveled, and his clothes were a mess. His red tie hung low around his neck, his shirt tail hung out of his trousers, and the two sides of his belt flapped around.

His eyes, though, almost reminded me of someone—possibly the person I may have been with. I looked into his eyes and saw them shift left and right, trying to look around to make sure he wasn't seen.

There was no guilt in his eyes. Why was I looking for guilt? There was no sadness, no happiness, no hate, no... nothing. There was no emotion whatsoever. He was on auto-drive.

He moved deeper into the darkness and headed for the elevated railroad tracks that I saw in the distance. His steps were timed and measured. His breathing steadied and metered. He walked deliberately toward the elevated tracks. He never shifted his load in his arms, even when he stepped up the small hill.

He turned right and proceeded down the tracks. For some reason, I was drawn to continue with him and his package. He stepped onto each of the boards holding the rails down. There was a missing board along the way, and he stepped over the area without adjusting his stride.

The track took him toward a rail bridge. He continued stepping from one railroad tie to the next, halting midway across before turning to his right, toward the edge.

I looked down to see that it was a long way down to an area of a black flowing mass. I believed it to be water because I could hear waves breaking on its banks and then sloshing back to the center.

I was somehow able to maneuver myself to his front side so I could see what he was carrying in his arms.

The cradled mass almost looked recognizable to me. The hair was dark and mussed up. Its clothing was tattered and soiled, and its skin was scratched, bloodied, and bruised.

I leaned in and looked into its eyes and then remembered... everything.

It all came back in a scream. I knew who I was and what he did to me. The ripping of my clothes, his pressure against my hands, the weight of him on my neck, the violations inside me, and the back of my head slamming against a rock.

"NOOOOOOOOOOO! Bastard! Put me down! Don't do this! I'm still alive! I know it!" I swung at him and hit nothing. I started screaming at myself. "Wake up! Don't let him do this to me." I broke down and started to cry. "Please don't do this."

I saw my arm move. It looked more like a twitch, but it was a movement. I know Ken saw and felt it. I looked at him in the hope that he would let me go.

He did.

As my body hit the chilled waters below, I could feel my gut wrench, my lungs seized, and my heart pierce with blades. Even though I was no longer in my body, I could feel the last moments of my life that my body was going through.

The screams and pain inside me turned my sorrow to anger, and I wanted to find the source of my newly discovered rage.

Ken.

I turned away from looking at where my body began to disappear and moved down the fast-moving Trinity River. I could no longer see him, but I knew he was there. I wanted to find him, hurt him, tear him apart, and then kill him.

"Do you really want to do that, Rachel?" A voice came from beyond my sight.

"I want him to suffer. I want him to beg and plead at my feet for forgiveness. I want his life to come crashing down on him." I answered the voice. I did not know if it was my voice or someone else's.

"That is the anger of the moment, child. I know you want one thing more than that."

I was seething and spitting curse words. How dare this voice tell me what I wanted? I turned my head around looking for the owner of the voice. I shouted into the air, "And what would that be?"

"Justice."

She stepped out of nowhere. A woman I'd never laid eyes on before. Someone I would have never forgotten, even if I had. Golden-brown hair, deep bronzed skin, a simple white dress, and green piercing eyes that pulsed with light.

"More than anything else, you want to see him pay for what he did to you, because in his mind, he believes that he did nothing wrong. He acted like a child with a new toy. He got to play with it, then damaged it, discarded it into his toy box, and then went off to find another new toy to play with." She placed her right hand on my shoulder and said, "You, Rachel, want justice."

I crumpled to the ground and said, "Yes. I want him to pay for what he did. I want to see him when they come for him. I want to see his eyes when it's his time to die. I want him to know he cannot get away from what he's done. I want him to think every day about me and what he did."

"I will make sure you get that opportunity, Rachel. He may have already sealed his fate that night, because of something small and unnoticeable."

"What would that be?"

"When the time comes, you will be there to see it. You have my promise. For now, I would enjoy a few minutes of your company if you do not mind." She turned her hand up and placed it in front of me.

She assisted me up. "Let us start with a change of clothes, shall we? And then let's go find this hunter of yours. For when it comes to matters of life and death, he is but a cub to me."

There was something I saw in her eyes that froze my insides and made me understand that all of her promises would be kept.

"You know my name, but I do not know yours. What is it?"

"What name would you like to give me?"

I stood there looking at her. I shook my head. "I have no name for you."

"No worries, dear Rachel. Eventually, someone will give me one. I had one for a while, but they moved on to the next Realm."

"I have to ask. If you know what I'm feeling, and you have an idea of what will happen to him, do you read minds and feelings of others? Are you able to see the future?"

"I did not have to read your mind. I know quite well what it is that you really want. Very well indeed. And with your question about the future, no, I am not able to see that, but things have a way of working themselves out."

Her eyes went out of focus for a moment, as if she were remembering something, and then they focused back on me. "I promised you a change of clothes. Let's see what we can do."

She turned and faced me. "I want you to close your eyes." I did. "Now think of what you want to wear. Think of the kind of clothes you would feel safe in. Something to show your inner strength in an outward appearance."

I placed an image in my mind. "Good. Good. That is perfect, Rachel. Now open your eyes and look at yourself."

In front of me, a mirror appeared that, and I could see myself in it. "What you see, Pamela, is the look I chose for myself."

Except for one slight change.

I looked at the woman. She nodded knowingly as I reclosed my eyes and thought.

When I reopened them, the wound on my head was gone, but the small images of the bruises on my neck remained.

The woman said, "You healed the damage to your head, why not your neck?"

"I want a reminder of what happened. I also want something to show him when he sees me again."

The lady in white slowly nodded. "I understand. Are you ready to watch the end of this story?"

"Will it happen soon?"

"Sooner or later. What I will do is allow you to walk the path beside him. To watch what he does, how he acts, and how he will fail.

Once the conclusion happens, there will be a way for you to go where I came from. From there, your parents will come and collect you when it is their time."

Tears grew. "I get to see them again?"

"If that is what you wish. When they get to my Place to meet you, you can greet them with open arms and tears of joy."

My tears flowed downwards and around my cheeks. "I want that."

"We are in agreement, correct?"

"Yes."

Her voice then lost any sense of compassion. "Close your eyes. Focus on him. Go find him. I will see you at the conclusion."

I had never heard a voice that was so determined, so cold. At the same time, she placed a conviction inside me to go forward with my plan.

And with that, she was just…gone.

~*~

I did what she said to do, and there I was, walking next to him. I stood there as he washed and cleaned his car. I sat next to him as he drove home. He memorized, repeatedly, what he was going to say when everyone questioned him.

I even lay next to him when he went to bed.

The next few days there were a flood of questions, as he expected. I heard the lies spew out of his charmed lips. To his credit, he never skipped a beat and never changed his story. He told them how he and I got into a verbal argument. He talked about how I got out of the car and walked away. He said that he tried to get me back into the car and how I refused his offer, punched the door slightly, hence the small dent on his new red car, and stormed away in a new direction.

The girls at school, who were enamored of him, now didn't want to walk next to him, sit near him, or stand by him. They felt funny, nervous, or weird about something around him.

The guys at school just left him alone. If he closed into a group of them, they would disperse quickly.

A hunter cannot hunt if he cannot hide.

My body had been missing now for days without any word of my possible whereabouts. My parents begged, pleaded, and cried out to the community to help find me. Ken watched as the news covered the story. Again, I saw he had no reaction to my mother's plea. He walked up, turned the television off, and continued with his day.

The police went to his home and to the school asking questions. They brought him to the police station for even more questions. He stuck to his story word for word.

This went on for weeks. The story left the airwaves. The police slowed down their investigation. The students stopped talking about it. Life went on for everyone, except me.

And my parents.

They were relentless. Not only did they go after him with both barrels, but they also brought in the hounds, in the form of private investigators. They dug out every piece of information on Ken's world they could find. I couldn't have been prouder of my mom and dad.

With the hounds circling and my parents hunting, the edges of Ken started to fray. He started to have trouble sleeping. Then he couldn't eat. His eyes, which were dead and focused started shifting wildly. He twitched at certain sounds and words.

The girls at the school started talking about him, about his temper, his need for control, his cold eyes. They talked about narrowly escaping moments of discomfort. They believed that they were saved because they were always around other people and students during those times.

Then it all stopped.

For more than a month, there was nothing chasing after him. The hounds were gone. I thought my parents went hunting in a new direction. The whispers dissipated into the night. Ken started to relax. He slept and ate right again. He believed he had won.

Then they found my body further downstream in the Trinity River from where I was last seen by Ken.

And with that, they burned the fields, brought in more hunters, tracked, and buried Ken in a mountain of ever-growing questions and outright accusations. The layers of Ken peeled away, showing the spoiled little twisted piece of shit coward that he was. Even with all the mounting pressure pushing down and around him, he kept his story straight.

God knows how.

I felt that he might continue to slip through their fingers. That, with everything they piled on to him, he would still escape his punishment. I thought that he might never be caught, and I would have to watch him possibly do it again to someone else in the future if he were not stopped.

Then suddenly, the police brought something to Ken's family house. It was a search warrant to re-examine the car. They found on the left side, just above the hairline, there was a strange bruise that didn't make any sense to the examiner. It happened before my death and wasn't shaped like anything that they already ruled out. They wanted to look once more in the car to see if something could've caused the damage.

With photos of the damaged area on my head, they rummaged through the newly shined car. They had their fingers on every inch of the car. The buckles on their belts placed scratches into the paint. Their sprays that detect blood stained the leather seat and dashboard.

They turned his car inside out. I smiled for the first time since my death. I hoped that the red car would be shredded and dismantled. I also saw the look in Ken's eyes as his beloved little toy got clawed and mauled by the hunters. It was priceless.

"Time to go, little warrior."

I turned around to look to see where the voice came from and saw nothing. "It's not over yet."

"Yes, it is."

I turned back to the car.

Ken took his time cleaning up the car to hide anything that might convict him. In the months afterward, he continually cleaned it to make sure that he missed nothing.

Everything was perfect.

There were no scratches, fingerprints, or anything else besides that small dent on the door that had been explained away.

Or so he thought.

Inside the passenger's side door, deep in the pocket that was on the door, and underneath the CDs he stored there, was something he never saw or touched. The item fit perfectly with my injury on the left side of my head and the indent on top of the door.

It was the blue barrette that I wore in my hair that night.

~*~

"After that," Rachel said, "there was no need for me to be there. I knew there was nothing he could say, do, or smile his way out of. I left him there. The area around me melted away like an oil painting when turpentine was splashed on it."

"Is that it?" Pamela said. "You just moved on? You weren't pissed off anymore? He took your life, he got caught, and that's it?"

Rachel smiled. "You don't understand the Place we are going to. There are a few things that will happen once he leaves his life."

"And that would be?"

"I will be there to greet him. He will face me. I will face him. I will tell him goodbye, and I will walk away."

"Is that it?"

"No. After that, he will meet something else. You've heard me mention the lady in white?"

"Yes."

"That's Rain. She collects the lost children, watches over them, and releases them to their loved ones when they arrive.

"She is not the only One here. There is another One who collects the selfish abusers of their lives. There are those who ended their lives, not because of compassion and sacrifice, but because of greed, loathing, and depravity. It comes and They collect them Then They consume them into Themselves.

"Then there is another. They come and collect the murderers. Those who greedily take a life away for their own gains, to fuel their hatred, and to take something special from others. They collect them and then places them into a cycle that relives the last moments of their victim's death from their point of view. Over and over, repeatedly.

"That is the One Ken will meet after I walk away from him."

Pamela stood motionless, thinking about what she would like to do. "I don't want to follow that thing that mauled and killed me. It is a nightmare I don't want to relive. I don't need to see him when he's dragged off to Hell. This is my Hell, and I just want to leave here." She closed her eyes and thought about the state of her clothes.

Then, everything that was damaged was not damaged anymore. She looked like she did before that moment with him.

"Where do you want to go?" Rachel asked.

"I want to go where you said this Rain lives, and I would like to meet her. But first, can we go to my home and see my parents? Even if it's just for a little while? I would like to be with them while they grieve for me."

"That can be arranged."

Pamela grasped Rachel's hand. "I would also like it if you would come with me. I could use a good friend to lean on, and I would like a shoulder to cry on."

Rachel squeezed Pamela's hand back and smiled. "I'd like that. Thank you." She closed her eyes and sent out a thought. A door of light appeared in front of them. "Okay. Close your eyes, think of your parents, and step through."

Pamela did as she was told. The door shifted and pulsed. The light was warm, bright, and inviting. With Rachel in hand, Pamela went home.

Chapter Eight - Isaiah

As a Deification of Death, I understand the multiple layers of fear and its effect on Mankind. How they manage fear shapes who they are or what they can become. They can help themselves out of the darkness by confronting their own fears, or their fears can push them deeper under the covers because they do not want to know what truly lurks out there in the unknown.

There are some who let fear hinder them from accomplishing the remarkable in their lives. They idly stand by as others are being hurt because they fear that if they lend a hand, they could be dragged down into a lower level of life or class, and they too could receive the same punishment from the opposition.

Some fear that others will not accept them if they come clean about who they are or what they feel. They fear they will not be accepted by the masses who judge what is or is not normal, or that one person they respect might turn away and shun them if the truth is revealed.

Confronting and using fear can allow others to do spectacular, wondrous things. They understand there may be a chance of pain, but the accomplishment of the task may be well worth the risk. Even in the face of overwhelming fear, they would take a breath, open their eyes, and step forward to continue doing what they believed they were doing to help others.

Challenging fear could also make them do impulsive and stupid things, resulting in injury or death. They believe that if they do something monumentally ridiculous and survive, they will have their fifteen minutes of fame and become immortal in the eyes of others and the camera. Most of the time, they will end up as the butt of the joke, a laugh on a late-night talk show, or just a smear of blood wrapped around a telephone pole.

Some fears come from a basic lack of understanding. Prejudices, stereotypes, and hate stem from this. They feel that some of those around them, in their limited sight, are somehow inferior to their way of thinking. They believe that because of a difference in skin color, others are not human but some sort of substandard animal. If they do not have the money or resources, their upbringing must be insufficient. If they are ill, tired, or physically unable to perform the tasks others can easily accomplish, then they have no place in the scheme of life. This way of thinking belongs to a sick, small-minded, hateful creature that should be pitied, not hated, because they themselves are fearful of even the idea of change.

Acute fears and phobias can have an impact on some. Their hearts and minds cannot mentally manage or physically confront what is before them. They retreat into themselves instead of meeting their fears head-on. For them, fear is instantaneous and life-altering. In extreme cases, it can be life-ending.

~*~

"This is Velesia Del Toro, reporting live on the scene of a three-alarm inferno. This apartment complex fire has been raging for the past ten minutes. The crew and I arrived as the first fire trucks were arriving. The winds are blowing here, with gusts reaching up to thirty miles per hour. Many people have fled the apartment complex, but there are fears that there may still be others inside."

~*~

His name was Isaiah. I found him in a bedroom filled with black and gray smoke while surveying the fiery building for possible opportunities to save a pair of young girls trapped higher up in the ever-growing inferno.

Isaiah was a healthy, shaven-headed Black man with a swimmer's physique. He wore sweatpants, running shoes, and a long-sleeved shirt. He was huddled against the bed's headboard. His eyes were wide open with a vacant stare. His chapped lips were parted just enough to let his last breath escape. His mind had given into the fear, and he simply…stopped.

I looked over his body for physical damage and found none. I watched his mind and spirit pass by me, and within the time of a single human heartbeat, I entered and took control of his body.

I decided I needed this body to complete my mission. I, Rain, the Deification of Death, had come there to save the girls, if I could, but the odds of me succeeding this time were heavily against me.

I have done this a few times when the right set of circumstances avail themselves to me. But to complete such a task requires that the people I choose must be in the right place, that the distance between my host and my objective must be manageable, and the timing must be exact for the life-saving task to succeed — otherwise, I would fail.

I have never taken failing well.

There would be no guarantee that it would work, but the rewards greatly outweighed the risks. If I succeeded in my task, or even if I failed, the decision would weigh heavily on my soul and thoughts. I knew I was doing nothing wrong by trying to do what was right.

I have learned from past experiences that when I take possession and animate a hallowed body, I will feel the damage that I cause to it.

The last thing this body knew was the fear of the coming flame. Isaiah and I share that particular phobia, whether it was warranted or not.

I, myself, am a product of both hate and the touch of the flame.

If I enter the body in trepidation, I could accelerate the remnants of the body's fear, and it would block me from entering. If I ever become separated from the body, it would not allow me to return to it. I wanted to make sure neither of these scenarios happened.

With that, the body and I became one.

~*~

I forced myself to wake up and take control of my body when the adrenaline hit. I took a deep, hard intake of air and coughed from the smoke. I held strong and waited for the energy to pass. The flames reached the bed at that moment, and I felt the heat.

I rolled off the bed and stood up. I could feel the heat coming from the floor. I moved toward the door, and a piece of cinder dropped from the ceiling, hitting me on my left forearm. The shirt and I took damage. I jerked and held my arm close to me as I left the bedroom.

The living room was engulfed in thick black and gray smoke. I could see flashes of light caused by the whipping flames, crackling wood, and electrical sparks. I searched for the safest course to the outer door of his apartment, but I could see nothing. The hot smoke choked and burned as it entered my lungs. I dropped to the floor and tried to get below the smoke.

I looked around to see if I could traverse the obstacles. I saw the table legs and chairs to my right. That was the direction of the kitchen and where the exit was. On the left were large shards of shattered glass shelves, smoking wood towers, and what remained of the television. In front of me was a plastic-melted, noxious-smelling burnt clump of furniture.

I skimmed quickly across the floor to the kitchen. I turned around the bend of the peninsula and could see the metal door. I knew it would be hot to the touch.

I got up to my knees and pulled at the shirt's sleeve. The stitching and the torso of the shirt separated, and I wrapped it around my hand before I reached for the handle.

Even with the shirt's fabric, more synthetic than cotton, I could feel the heat on my hand as I turned the knob. I jerked it to the right and yanked the door open. I left the inferno and crawled directly into Hell.

~*~

"Black and gray smoke is currently rolling out of every open window of the building. The fire and police departments have set up barriers to keep the people watching and our camera crew out of harm's way. You can look around you can see the loss of where they once lived echoing in their eyes."

~*~

There was less smoke in the hallway than in the apartment, but it made the scene even more horrifying. In the Fall, the seasonal changes always brings out feelings of calmness and peace for me, with the oranges, yellows, and red hues. They are always a welcome sight.

But the images I faced were not. The colors in the hallway did not warm my heart. Instead, they darkened my hopes of success. Because of my own personal past nightmares, I was afraid of the colors the inferno painted before me.

In the dark areas, images of twisted and distorted demons appeared. Horns, claws, and jaws, with black smoke billowing around me, blocked my intended path. I could almost hear the laughter and taunts of the creatures that should not exist in the realm of the Living.

It spoke in a language through the creaking, crackling, and breaking sounds around me. I knew what it was saying:

107

'They are mine. You are no match for me. Turn away. I will take the living with me. Abandon that body. Return to what you do.'

I steeled my will. I knew I had to make it to the stairs on the other side of this visual nightmare.

To get through this, I had to rid myself of every negative thought and focus solely on the task at hand. I looked directly at my objective and willed myself to ignore the pain.

I focused and ran into the fiery hall. I crossed my arms and covered my eyes to protect them from the soot and heat. The fear of pain was gone. The hate of the fire would not stop me. The despair of thinking I would be too late to save them was gone. The only thing left was the hope of getting through the corridor.

There could be no emotion involved, or I would have failed, and I do not take failure well.

As I passed through the doorway, I stumbled and fell onto the metal and concrete step. I felt my right kneecap crack. I tried to ignore the grinding, popping pain and moved on. It was then that I realized the entire back of the shirt was on fire, melting onto my skin.

Screams of pain shattered my focused calm. I dropped to my back to put out the fire, only to feel more pain as the burned flesh touched the floor.

~*~

"It is believed that there may be children in one of the upper apartments of the complex. Reports say that two children haven't been accounted for. The fire department is unable to go inside because of the intensity and heat of the blaze.

We are not sure if there is any way of saving...

Did we just hear a scream!? Did that come from inside the building!?"

~*~

I told myself I had to keep moving and get up the stairs. I rolled over from my burnt back, forced myself to stand, and continued up the stairs.

I couldn't breathe. My back screamed every time each muscle twitched, and my cracked knee buckled from the pain.

When I reached the top floor, I was so exhausted, all I wanted to do was give up and let the burning inferno consume me.

That's when I heard her.

It started off as a murmur in the distance. It was barely audible over the noises of the building's fiery crackles and the hallowed echoes of heated air causing ear barotrauma. I swallowed to clear my hearing.

I heard it once again: "Help us*cough*please."

Seven doors lay before me: three on the left, four on the right. They were in the apartment furthest to the right. I moved forward with all the speed I could muster.

Every step I took toward my goal, the door felt as if it was getting further from my reach. The fire and the smoke played Keep Away with me. The intake of smoke and the lack of oxygen muddled my mind and vision.

The hallway I moved down was the fire's own private broiler. The walls warped, and the paint and the floor were melting. The tiles must have been made of plastic because they now looked like pools of bubbling and sizzling ooze. When one of the bubbles erupted, it released small, noxious balls of exploding flames.

As I stepped onto the shimmering plastic floor of gel, it surrounded my foot and melded with my shoes. It collected, combined, and weighed my feet down. I could feel the heat through the shoes, searing my feet. The plastic's hold affected my balance and

109

my speed. I also knew I could not lose the shoes. If I did, the plastic would rip, grab, and tear the skin off the bone.

By sheer will, I did not fall to the ground. My hope was dwindling as fast as my body was dying. I braced myself against the wall and pulled myself down the hallway by the outer door frames. I avoided the metal doors themselves. I could see the heat pulsing off them.

When I reached the final door, I was so filled with pride, so consumed by the accomplishment, that I grabbed the handle without thinking about the consequences.

I ripped my hand away immediately. The scream that escaped me was reserved for souls ripped, devoured, and absorbed by the Suicide Death. The decimation of a soul is gut-wrenching.

I remember every person I condemned to Them. I remember every scream that followed.

The skin and blood I left on the knob sizzled, blackened, and turned to ash in mere moments. I tore a strip from the remaining fabric of my shirt and wrapped it around my seared, bloody hand. I took another strip, wrapped it around my left hand, and placed it on the knob.

I leaned into the process of opening the door, but it did not budge. The door had expanded from the heat and was wedged tight.

I had to get in there. I would not let a piece of metal stand in the way of saving those children's lives. I refused to fail when I was so close.

I shut down the human emotions screaming in my mind—telling me that I am tired, and I needed to give up this foolish mission. I closed my thoughts that told me it was time to leave this body, collect the children, take them to the Forest, and allow them to wait their parents' arrival.

I took half a step back, supported myself with my better leg, and lifted the burning, plastic-dipped foot. I let out a scream of defiance and kicked the metal door with everything I had to jar it free.

~*~

"We are still waiting for confirmation to find out if everyone has been evacuated from the building and if the children have been found. As you can see behind me, the lights of the fire can be seen in every window. Smoke and flames are pouring out from the roof. I don't know how much longer the roof will hold before its collapse.

"Did you hear that? Did anyone else hear a scream? Oh my God! There's still something in there!"

"Turn the camera toward the third floor!

"As you can see, the glass from those upper windows has been blown out, and shards are raining down below.

"For those just tuning in, a massive apartment fire has been raging for the last fifteen to twenty minutes. The fire department has now declared the building a complete loss. They've called for their men to pull back and let the fire burn, even before they could set up their hoses.

"But just a few moments ago, and once again, I swear I heard what sounded like a scream coming from inside the inferno. It seems impossible to hear anything over the roar of the flames, the firefighters shouting orders, and the fire trucks blaring their sirens. But somehow, there was an unmistakable scream cutting through all of that noise. We all turned our heads at once to locate it."

~*~

The kick did what it needed to do. It jolted the door enough to swing open. My foot, already suffering from second and third-degree burns, screamed in pain as the blisters burst on impact.

111

The slight temperature variation and difference in pressure between the hallway and apartment rushed into the room, pushing out the compressed air and created a blast furnace of scalding heat. The high winds from outside dragged in ash and burning embers, throwing them straight into my face and eyes, blinding me.

The door slammed back against my right shoulder as I tried to move into the room. It rebounded off me just enough to keep it from sealing shut. I felt my way through the apartment, using every sense but sight.

I already knew where Sarah and Amy were hiding from the moment I took possession of Isaiah's body. I knew the layout.

I needed to pass through another door on my left, but what wasn't in the vision was the burning kitchen table I walked straight into.

I stumbled over the pile of smoldering wood in the middle of the floor. The jagged, charred edges stabbed into my skin at multiple points, adding more blood to the growing mess. My time in this body was running out.

I extended my arm, found the door to the girls' bedroom, and pushed it open.

With my left leg, I pushed off, dragging my right leg behind me, and staggered into the room.

In a voice that was not my own, I called out, "Sarah? Amy? Where are you?"

There was no answer.

I raised my voice, trying to cut through the sounds of the building burning. "Girls, I am here to get you out! Can you answer me?"

A cough came from ahead of me a small, strained voice. "Here... here."

"Can you see me?" I asked.

"A little."

"I cannot see. Can you put your hand out and touch mine?"

"You're too far away."

"Can you come closer?"

"I'm not leaving Amy. She's not waking up."

"I understand, Sarah. Just tell me how to reach you, and I will get you and your sister out of here. I promise."

Sarah coughed again, and I could hear how much trouble she was having breathing.

"Sarah!" I spoke directly to her, louder and more authoritative, hoping to shake her enough to respond.

It worked.

"Here. We're here!"

"Where?"

"A little more." I reached to my right, waving my arm around, hoping to brush my finger against hers. "The other way!"

I heard her scream and quickly swung my arm in the opposite direction.

"Stretch your arm out a little more, Sarah! Tell me when I get close!"

After a few moments of reaching as far as I could, I brushed her fingertips. That gave me the location I needed.

Sarah gripped my thumb, and I winced at the pain from the burnt skin. But I did not pull my arm away. "Hold onto Amy, and I will pull you both to me."

Sarah moved toward me, and when we were next to each other, I pulled both of them against my chest. "Is there a blanket nearby?"

"Yes," Sarah replied, followed by a cough from the smoke.

"I have you both, but I need you to grab it and bring it to us."

I felt Sarah shift around, extending her hand and arm toward something. A moment later, a large blanket brushed my face. "Here," she said.

"Good. I need your help to cover you and your sister up. This may help keep the ash from hurting you."

I felt her nod. "You said you can't see, right?" she asked, sounding concerned.

"No. The ash burned my eyes."

"How are you going to get us out if you can't find the way?"

"I will do my best. I have a good memory."

After a brief pause, Sarah said, "I'll keep my face uncovered and tell you where to go."

I was not going to argue with her. I tilted my head down, signaling a positive response.

"I am going to try to stand up with you two in my arms. Move your face close to my ear so I can hear you."

I lifted myself and the girls off the floor. Ten different screams filled my mind from various spots on my body. The worst pain was from the shards of glass embedded in my thigh.

I moved toward what I hoped was the direction of the front door. Sarah guided me by whispering in my ear, telling me which way to go. She helped me avoid the table and the sharp edge of a countertop.

When we moved into the hallway, I heard Sarah cry out and bury her face in my shoulder.

~*~

"I'm still just outside the scene of this horrendous event. With these high winds, there's no way to control the fire. As you can see, the flames are now escaping from the rooftop. The fire department is calling it a total loss and is now focused on preventing the flames from spreading to nearby trees and buildings by spraying the trees down with water.

"Twenty-six families have been displaced. There are reports that not everyone has been accounted for, and they are still combing through the area for two children who are still missing. Additionally, we've heard screams coming from inside the building, so there may still be others in there somewhere."

~*~

I knew what the hallway had looked like before I lost my vision, though I suspected it had not improved in the last few minutes. I could feel the heat on my face and hear the creaks, cracks, and crashes surrounding us. The air was thick with the acrid taste of soot and melted tile.

I needed Sarah's sight to guide us. With her face buried in my shoulder, she could not help. "Sarah," I said, "I need your help."

She choked back a sob, sniffled, and coughed. I felt her head lift slightly. "Turn to your left. There's a burning piece of wood in the middle of the hallway. You need to get over it."

"Thank you."

"I want my mom and dad. I want Amy to wake up."

"Soon, Sarah. Soon," I murmured. Another creak and crash echoed ahead. "We need to get out of here now. Hold on tight and guide me."

The pain was overwhelming, and I felt myself on the verge of collapsing. Blood loss was making me dizzy, but I knew I couldn't give up. I gathered every ounce of strength and pressed forward.

Sarah's voice gave me direction—left, right, stop, go. Her guidance kept us moving down the hallway.

A piece of burning wood bounced off my back, pushing me forward. The back of my shoulder slammed into the doorframe near the stairwell.

Going up the stairwell had been treacherous when my sight was intact. Going down the stairs blind would be much worse.

"Sarah, tell me when I am near the steps," I said, trying to keep my voice steady.

"I can't see anything. I don't know where the steps are."

"You must see them so we can get down. Let me lower us so you can find them."

"Okay." I knelt as low as I could, giving her space to see. "I see them now."

"Good." I exhaled with relief and coughed from inhaling the smoke. "Tell me where to go."

I moved my feet in the direction Sarah directed. I took quick, small steps to avoid tripping or falling down the stairwell.

Sarah stopped me with a gentle press against my body. I reached out with my foot, searching for the next step. When I found it, I continued cautiously down.

I did not grab the railings or move my arms around for balance because I had to keep the girls close—precious cargo to deliver out of this inferno.

The heat and smoke surged up through the stairwell, desperately searching for an escape. We were right in its path. The stairwell had become a chimney for the fire below.

We moved down and around the stairs from the third floor to the second. I counted the steps when I went up—twenty steps between each level. Now, descending, I counted again, hoping there would not be any surprises.

Sarah directed me to turn right again and continue down the next flight. I could hear the creaking, snapping, and crunching of the building around us. I hoped the stairs would hold up for those last twenty steps down and walk down the corridor, to our safe exit.

As I started the last set of stairs, I pulled the girls closer and focused on the rhythm of the stairs. Moving forward, step by step, I made my way toward the safety I could almost taste.

I heard the sound of a chunk of rock crashing down to our left. I felt the pieces bounce off my leg and listened to the fragments tumble down the lower steps.

The final steps turned into a shower of rocks, wood, and metal. The crash grew louder, closer—each piece falling with more force than the last. The entire stairwell was coming down around us.

I prayed silently, desperately for just a few more moments to finish my task.

My answer was a heavy thud on my back, and everything went black.

~*~

I stood there, looking down at Isaiah's lifeless body. His legs were pinned beneath a pile of rubble; the weight of the debris caused the body to crash into the ground and dispel me. I stood frozen, arms still positioned as if I was still holding the girls.

Sarah and Amy were below the fallen body of Isaiah. Because of my last thoughts of keeping the girls safe, in my final moments of instinct, the body cradled them, protecting them from the crash down.

I wanted to get back to them. I tried to return, to merge back into Isaiah's body.

But the connection was gone.

I knew this would happen, but that did not stop me from trying. I was desperate to grasp on to anything that would tether, any thread that might let me attach myself back to him.

But my entry was denied.

There was nothing I could do. I had failed them. I could no longer keep them safe and alive.

"I've seen better days, haven't I?" A voice came from behind me, devoid of any sarcasm.

I turned to find Isaiah standing a few steps behind me. He was no longer the image of the broken man I left lying on the ground. He stood tall, his strong shoulders unshaken, the way I had seen him when I first arrived, a tall Black man with a strong set of shoulders that I needed to save the world.

He stepped toward me. His stride was purposeful, and there was a sense of resolve in his movement as he came closer.

"What are you doing here? Your time here is over. It is time for you to be elsewhere."

"I did go to the next Place," Isaiah replied, his voice calm but firm. "The Ones who met me welcomed me with open arms and smiles wide. They explained to me what you were doing. They said your sacrifice didn't go unnoticed, and they helped you where they could. They extended Sarah's voice to guide you, to give you hope. They made sure your task was fulfilled. And when I asked if I could return to help you find the way and they allowed it. They wanted to make sure that your task to save them was complete."

I stared at him; the pain of defeat weighed heavily in my chest. "I can no longer enter your body."

"No, but they said I could to finish the task you started."

I shook my head. "I do not think you will be able maintain control for long. You might get back inside but the pain from all the damage would push you back out. The burns, the breaks, the trauma..."

"It's my body," Isaiah interrupted her, "and it knows me. I believe it has just enough strength left for me to do this."

"Be that it might be true, but I fear we might be too late to save them

Isaiah spoke; his expression was resolute. "We both know no time has passed since you were expelled from my body. 'In the threads between the fabric of time, is where the Angels roam.'" His words were familiar and profound. "The Place of In-between is a place of thought and void of even the idea of time itself. So, what are we right now, if not Angels?"

Isaiah smiled. "I wrote that a while ago, never quite knowing what it meant until this moment." He stood in contemplation, his mind reaching for something deeper. After a moment, he spoke again. "I'm reminded of something else I once wrote. 'It is Chaos that commands the threads of the In-between. Order stitches those threads together creating seconds of time. Skipping to one stitch after another is called continuity.' We are definitely in the one of the in-between moments."

Isaiah's gaze shifted to the environment around us. The damage from the destruction hung still, frozen in time—concrete crumbled, iron rebar twisted, and smoldering wood remained motionless. His eyes focused on a single ember suspended in the air. He lifted his hand, reaching for it. His finger passed through the image. The ember showed no trace of movement from Isaiah's action.

"And right now, Chaos is most definitely in command here, at this moment," he said, a hint of awe in his voice.

He surveyed the almost stationary flames. He looked back at me with conviction. "It's time to move things forward."

He paused and met my eyes, the weight of his promise clear. "I won't let them die. I promise you. I will hold on long enough to do that. They deserve to live, to change the world if they choose to do so."

"One life at a time. One moment that changes everything," I replied, my thoughts lingering on the weight of his words.

I took a breath, considering the act he'd just performed. "What did you see when you looked at that burning ember, Isaiah?"

He smiled a boyish grin. "Everything." He moved toward his body, then stopped and cocked his head in my direction. "By the way, The Oher Ones said she will be a wonderful choice when the time comes. You've made them all proud of what you've done and what you continue to do." And with that, he took a leap of faith and returned back into his body.

Within the span of one of Isaiah body's heartbeat, I once again became the observer of the story. I was no longer able to help him or the girls.

~*~

The first thing I heard was Isaiah screaming from the damage I had done to his body. It crushed my heart.

He was blind, his leg crushed, his skin charred, his hands and feet blistered, and what was left of his melted shirt grafted onto his skin. No mere mortal could endure what had happened to his body.

But he did endure it.

He leaned back and struggled with the debris on his leg. His body tented over the girls. Hell, and Damnation would have to get through him to even touch them, and he would not let that happen.

Isaiah slid up against the girls and tried to stand on his not-so-good left leg. I stood there, my breath held, my nails digging into my

120

palms, watching every twitch of his muscles as he worked to get onto his feet.

He was shaky on his first step but made the adjustments. He tightened his grip on the girls and moved forward.

His knees buckled, but he did not fall. He screamed in pain but did not crumble. Pieces of the ceiling fell around him and struck him multiple times, but he did not topple. He did not let go of Sarah and Amy.

I saw Isaiah take the last few slow and deliberate steps toward the exit door. I did not know how many steps he still had to take, but I knew he would take them all and deliver Amy and Sarah to their family before his body expired.

~*~

Fear determines what happens to us. It is how we deal with it that makes us who and what we are. There are those who let it hinder them from accomplishing remarkable things in their lives by standing still.

Others overcome it and become something more than they were before. Sometimes, they accomplish what Man thought they could not and should not be able to do.

In the eyes of those who are witness to the impossible, they become Heroes and Saints.

His name was Isaiah.

I knew the girls' family would be there waiting for them. Their crushing sorrow and the loss that speared itself into their hearts would turn to pure joy, flooding their lungs, minds, and hearts.

I watched as the last of the apartment building collapsed around me. I heard the fire and the shadows in this inferno scream in defeat, through creaks, cracks, and crushing twisting metallic sounds. The howls of the wind, through the gaps in the rubble, created the sounds of demons being pulled back into Hell, in loss of Its prey.

No child would die at this place. It threw everything it had at Isaiah's body. Isaiah's and my flesh and hearts did not fail Sarah and Amy. I laughed a glorious cheer of satisfaction.

Death was denied. I was just fine with that.

~*~

"Tragedy is playing out before us here at the burning apartment complex, where we have just learned two children are unaccounted for. In a moment of heroism by a neighbor, an unconscious woman, overcome by smoke, was taken out of the building. What was not known at the time was that the unconscious woman's two daughters were still in the apartment. The husband, who you see there, returned home to find the structure burning and sought out the police and fire department for help. By then the building was too unsafe to enter. Our hearts go out to them, and our prayers are with the children, Sarah and Amy."

"We will keep you updated on the situation from the apartment fire later. Once again, the fire here has claimed at least two lives. From Coppell, I'm Velicia Del Toro. Back to you in the studio—"

"Oh my God and Heaven above! Look!"

"Wait a minute! Studio, keep the transmission going.

"A woman is screaming from the crowd and pointing to the fire. There's something going on. It looks as if somebody is coming out of the collapsing building. They are smoldering, struggling to move, and it looks as if they are carrying something tightly against their arms!"

Chapter Nine - Naomi

…As the kitten lay in her nice, warm bed, she spied a snowflake dancing in the frame of the large glass window across from her. She watched as it drifted toward the window's left edge, changed direction, and then disappeared below the windowsill.

Naomi leapt from her bed and padded over to the glass pane, eager to find the playful flake. As she approached, she spotted even more of the white wind dancers. They swirled and twirled like the first one, only to vanish somewhere below the window frame.

Naomi decided they must be playing a game of Tag or Keep Away. They looked like they were having so much fun, and she wanted to see more of it.

A wondrous idea came to her.

Whenever Naomi had an idea, her whiskers would twitch and tickle her cheeks, making her giggle out loud.

The kitten knew that if she could get down the stairs that she would see even more of the dancing snowflakes through the lower windows before they disappeared into the snowy white yard. She had to move very kitten-carefully.

She could hear the two silly dogs bumbling around downstairs, making anxious noises as they waited to go outside and play in the snow. Since they were older than Naomi, the Humans allowed them to go out on their own.

But the Humans didn't let Naomi do the same.

Every time she got close enough to the door to make her escape, one of the Humans would scoop her up, bring her face close to theirs, kiss her on the nose, and say, "No, no, no." Then, they would place her back in one of her play areas.

~*~

Naomi made it all the way down the stairs and around the corner without being caught. The space between the stairs and the wall had a large enough window for her to watch what was happening outside.

She saw the silly dogs romping around before disappearing beyond the large area of trees. Naomi figured that something marvelous must be hidden beyond there, for the silly dogs always dash into the trees and vanish beyond them.

The two Humans exchanged words, clapped their hands together three times, made some strange gestures with their fingers, and then, after a grunt, one of them trudged off in pursuit of the dogs beyond the trees.

The two silly dogs would always return carrying their little trinkets, grinning from ear to ear. The Human who had gone after them looked exhausted from the chase, a deep frown etched across their face.

Both Humans shook their heads in disapproval, grabbed the silly dogs by the scruffs of their necks, and led them to the door, ordering them inside. The silly dogs tromped mud and leaves onto the floor, then raced up the stairs in a dogged hurry, bouncing off the walls as they bounded to the top of the house.

Knowing the kind of chaos the silly dogs could cause, the Humans rushed after them. In their confusion and concern, they left the door open just a kitten's paw width.

Naomi realized this was her best chance to finally accomplish the goal she had never been able to achieve.

The kitten slunk over to the bottom edge of the stairs, looking to see if the coast was clear, and then crept her way the doorway.

She reached the outside door just as she heard one of the Humans speaking aloud and walking back toward the stairwell.

Naomi knew it had to be now. If she waited a whisker's twitch longer, the Human would spot her, scoop her up into their arms, slam the door shut, and her chance would be gone.

She twisted her head back toward the outdoors, slid on her belly to the door, stretched out her paw, and nudged it open a little further. Then, with a leap, she sprang into the unknown.

The door swung shut behind her, and the light above flicked off just moments after her escape. She took a few tentative steps, then a couple more, pausing to see if she had been caught.

But when no Humans came after her, she knew—victory was hers.

A grin tried and failed to form on her cold lips, her breath curling in smoky wisps before her. Instead, her whiskers twitched so much she thought they might wriggle away on their own. She did all she could to keep from laughing out loud at the tickling sensation.

Naomi's eyes adjusted to the dark world before her. She wanted to see how far the snow stretched, so she stood tall on her hind legs and peered around, only to find the snow reached up to her belly.

Now, a cat's vision is unlike that of silly dogs or Humans. Cats can see past the shadows, detecting the slightest movement of a leaf or a drifting snowflake.

Naomi decided she would chase one of the funny little snowflakes floating lazily through the air, taking its time to settle on the ground. She knew she wanted to play with it, so she readied herself to pounce.

She lowered her chin, lifted her hindquarters, twitched her tail to match the rhythm of her whiskers, and locked her gaze on the exact spot where the flake would land.

The moment it touched the ground; Naomi leapt into action.

The trouble was her landing sent the flake—and all the others nearby flying into the air, she lost sight of her prey. Undeterred by the failure of capture, she focused on another flake and prepared for another attempt.

The merry Snowflake Chase continued on several more times before she finally admitted that the game was impossible to win though she had to admit, it was fun trying, nonetheless.

She scanned her surroundings, her whiskers twitching with curiosity. Then, her eyes landed on the spot where those silly dogs had run toward.

She was ready. It was time for her to see what lay beyond those trees.

~*~

The journey to the trees ended up being more problematic than Naomi had thought. The snow was already higher than her belly, and every time she jumped forward, the next snow hole she created was deeper than the one before.

After her fourth pounce, Naomi stood up to see that the snow now reached her neck, and she was still nowhere near her journey's end.

Her fur was cold and wet, as was the skin beneath it, but she was not going to let that stop her from getting past those trees. She wanted to bring back proof to show the Humans and those silly dogs that she could do everything they could and even more.

She pushed herself up past the opening of the snow hole and, lying on her belly, carefully slid on top of the snow. Stretching her front paws ahead, she pulled herself forward, trying not to create another kitten-sized hole to fall into.

After several attempts, she neared the trees. Her wet belly and paws no longer felt cold. She knew that within a few more pulls she would make it, so she continued on.

At the edge of the trees, she found that the snow was not as deep, and she could almost walk on the ground.

She used her sharp eyes to look around and to decide what to do next.

What she found was more trees, many of them larger than the ones beside her. She wanted to get past all the trees to see what was on the other side and knew the trees ahead of her would not stop her.

Her nose and lips were no longer cold, which she took as a good sign to continue on.

The snow was still paws-deep, but she could move faster now, weaving around and between some of the smaller trees in her way.

Naomi had a few missteps along the way, tripping over branches on the ground, but she quickly recovered each time.

The gusts of wind blew old leaves and tiny snowflakes past her face as she approached a tall, wide tree. She tried to see around it, hoping that there would be fewer trees once she passed it.

The winds strengthened, swirling snow and leaves around her, and a stick slapped her in the face. She flinched, but it did not hurt. She knew her final goal was just on the other side, and neither a stick nor a leaf would stop her from getting what she wanted.

Past the swirling winds of debris, she finally stood beside the great tree and looked ahead with her keen cat eyes.

She could not see beyond the tree line because of the heavy falling snow. Naomi saw only a thick white blanket draped in the air, and she did not know what to do next.

She thought about taking a few more steps to find something to bring back home, but she no longer wanted to go any further.

What she really wanted was just to get back home.

But she no longer knew where home was.

So, she sat down on her tail and tried to cry, but her small breaths wouldn't let her. Her sharp eyes felt heavy, wet, and stiff. The fingers on her paws barely moved, and her legs refused to move.

She was tired. She just wanted to sleep.

A few steps away, she spotted a pile of leaves and branches. It looked like a white-and-brown hill with a small hole just big enough for Naomi to crawl into and hide away from the wind.

A cave of leaves, sticks, and snow, just for her.

She wriggled into the open spot and curled up inside. There was another gap, just big enough for her eyes to peek through. It faced the place Naomi had almost reached— The open area, covered in snow.

She thought maybe she could sleep there for just a little while, and perhaps in the morning, she could go home.

Her whiskers would have twitched at the thought if they, and she, weren't so tired from the journey.

She stopped fussing, closed her eyes, and fell asleep.

~*~

There, in her little cave of sticks, leaves, and snow, Naomi opened her eyes and peered out of the entrance. A flickering light glowed a short distance away, something that hadn't been there before she fell asleep. The light expanded, shrank, shifted left and right, and made snapping sounds sharp enough for her ears to catch.

She understood that it was a fire, which meant warmth. She had only ever seen fire inside the glass-covered box in the Humans' living room. Many times, she had curled up there, with and without blankets.

She crept out of her cave, staying low in a crouch, then quietly made her way toward the fire. She knew only Humans could make fire, and she wanted to see who they were.

She took a few steps forward on to the snowy surface. Naomi moved to the right, took back two steps, held still, then continued forward again. She thought she was being incredibly sneaky, so much so that a joyful twitch of her whiskers made her giggle.

"Hello? Is there someone out there in the cold snow?" came a woman's voice, but the Human was hidden beyond the glow of the fire.

Naomi knew she had been discovered. She thought that if she made herself look large enough, she could scare this Human away and enjoy the fire all by herself.

She wriggled her tail, pumped her legs up and down, and inhaled a deep breath before leaping into view.

"Rowrrr," she growled as she landed, pouncing from the darkness into the warm, firelit area.

"Rowrrr," she said again, arching her back and slashing her tail through the air.

"That was a mighty roar. Am I to be afraid of you, oh mighty cat?" The voice behind the fire asked. "Or are you one of those silly dogs that jump around here?"

"I am no silly dog. I am a great and powerful cat."

"Goodness me! And what type of cat are you? Maybe a lion? Or are you some sort of cougar?"

"Of course not! I am a great and powerful Tiger. Cat."

"A tiger cat?! That IS something more powerful than any silly dog."

Naomi's whiskers twitched as she bared her fangs just below her upper lip.

"Well, your greatness," the female Human said, "how would you like to come around to the other side of the fire so I can see how impressive you are?"

Naomi circled to her left to see whom she was speaking to.

"My, oh my. You do show great courage coming around for me to see you."

Naomi moved another step forward and took a look at the Female Human sitting on a long wooden log, in an area where there was no snow on the ground.

Her dark skin and golden hair shimmered as the firelight reflected off them. Her dress was as white and bright as snow. She had bare feet, resting flat on the grassy ground. Her glowing green eyes never looked away from Naomi as the tiger cat approached.

"Yes, I do," Naomi said.

"Well then, Little Tiger, it is such a pleasure to meet you. You are brave and look very fearsome. How would you like to come closer to me and sit by the fire? You seem to be in no need of help, but I myself could use some protection from the darkness out there."

Naomi thought the Woman would not cause her any harm, but she also knew she needed to be cautious.

"I should be going back. The trail to my home is full of twists and turns, and if I weren't such a great tracker, I might lose my way."

"I understand. But if you sit with me, at least until sunrise, the trail may be easier to follow on your way back to your…"

"Humans."

"Yes. Humans and of course, those silly barking dogs."

"They think they are so much better than I am. Just wait until I get back and tell them I went farther than any of them, and that I even met you! I can't believe those Humans have such silly dogs, even if they were there before me."

Naomi paused before speaking again. "You know, I'm not afraid, but you do look very lonely, and it can be quiet out there in the dark." The kitten then said, "The way I thought I needed to go home wasn't right, so maybe I could sit with you for a little while? Maybe until sunrise?"

"It would be my honor to have you here with me, little one. We can keep each other warm and safe through the night."

Naomi stepped closer to the Woman in white. She found a spot clear of grass, close enough to the fire to stay warm. She took a few turns in a circle, then lay next to the log and the Woman's knees.

"Would you like me to sing to you, Little Tiger?"

"Yes, please."

The Woman smiled and began to sing in a whisper, "Hush, Little Baby."

After a few minutes, Naomi said, "My Humans would sing me that when I couldn't sleep. What else can you do?"

"What would you like me to do?" the Woman asked.

"Can you make some of the snowflakes bigger?"

"Of course I can." The snowflakes grew larger.

"Could you make a few of them dance around near me?"

Without a word from the Woman, one of the larger flakes, caught by a small breeze, drifted up to where the kitten lay.

The image of the snowflake reflected in both of Naomi's dark eyes before it drifted down toward her outstretched pads-up paw. When it touched one of her warm pads, it melted into a tiny droplet of water.

A tear escaped from Naomi's eye, slid down a whisker, fell onto the melted snowdrop, and merged with it. Together, they rolled off her paw and onto the ground.

Naomi closed her eyes and shivered, but not from the cold. "Can you help me go home?"

The wind and snow stopped as the Woman laid her hand on top of Naomi's head and brushed it gently across her forehead. "I wish that I could, but no. There are many things I can do, but that one is beyond even me, Little Tiger."

"Oh," Naomi said, as more tears dripped off her whiskers. "Do you think my Humans, or those silly dogs will be able to come and find me in the morning?"

The Woman said, "Yes, I am sure that they will. If you would like, you could stay near the warm fire until they arrive."

"Please," Naomi said as she curled into a tighter ball, cuddling her tail to her chest and resting her head on her paws.

The Woman laid a gray-and-white striped blanket over Naomi and lightly kissed the top of her head. "Rest now. They will be here soon enough."

~*~

"No, no, no," the boy in the gray bootie pajamas said, his dark complexion glowing in the dim light. "You're getting it all wrong. Her dress was made of rainbows, with long, bright gold hair."

132

"That's what Rain currently looks like now, Steele," Emily answered. "The story is called The Kitten and the Snow Queen."

She scanned the dark room, searching for the dark honey-haired girl curled up on the lowest level of a tall bunk bed near the glass fireplace. She wore a pair of gray-striped pajamas and held a matching blanket over her legs. The pajamas were the same her parents would dress her in at bedtime.

Lying next to her was a small stuffed brown tabby kitten she had named Naomi.

"This is your story I'm reading, Michelle. How should the Snow Queen look in your story?"

"Can you read it again, but this time put the rainbows in the gown, like he said? I would like to hear it again."

The roomful of children, sitting on the floor and bunk beds in a multitude of colorful pajamas, turned toward Emily with gleeful anticipation, eager for her to start the story over.

The curly blonde-haired girl with silver slippers sat at the front of the room, rocking gently in a chair, smiling. "Alright. One more time, with the rainbow dress. After that, Rachel can read you the next story she wrote, because I will have to leave. There is something I have to do with Rain."

She closed the book on her lap, flipped it back to the front cover, and opened it to the first page.

Above the book, a soft glow appeared in the shape of a small snow globe. The light inside was pale blue, and sparkling silver dots flowed downward toward the open book. Atop the book, an image of a small cat took form.

The Kitten and the Snow Queen.

"There once was a gray-striped kitten who..."

Chapter Ten - James

James's life was a life of songs. The symphony of his existence was shaped by every note, event, and person he encountered.

He was a son, a brother, a husband, a teacher, a father, and a man of simple means. Throughout the years, many songs he helped create ended, sometimes with violence. Other songs of his life carried on throughout the decades, becoming masterpieces that he replayed in his mind over and over. Many times, he wished he could still see and hear the original composition being built and growing, rather than just the version he played in remembrance.

In the early morning hours, while his wife, Sarah, slept, he would step out onto his dimly lit porch, sit in his chair with his guitar, and recall the haunting songs and moments of his past. For more than sixty years, his guitar had filled the air of the community he called home.

He experimented with different styles and genres of music while sitting on his porch. But when those songs ended, he always returned to the slow-hand blues. He believed that one day, an angel would come to his porch while he played.

Imagine his surprise when he saw two of them appear nearing his front step.

The first was a little blonde-haired girl. Her dress looked as if it had been sewn from gold. It fell just to her knees and was cinched at the waist with a silver ribbon tied into a bow at the back. Her socks were knee-high and white, and on her feet, she wore little silver slippers.

The woman was an awe-inspiring sight. She stood tall and proud, her shoulders pulled back in a stance of confidence. Her dress was creamy white and flowed as she moved. A myriad of colors appeared, each taking a moment to shine before fading as another took center stage.

James stopped playing the guitar, distracted by the vision.

"Please," the lady said, "do not stop playing on our behalf. It was very enjoyable. That was Robert Johnson's Crossroads Blues, correct?"

"Actually," James said with a slow drawl, his accent unmistakably Louisianan, "I was tryin' to play the Jimi Hendrix version and lost track of what I was doin' when you two showed up outta nowhere."

"I must say, from what I heard, it sounded incredible."

"Why, thank you, chère. Been havin' some issues with my hands of late, but they seem to be workin' just fine now tonight."

"I am glad I was here to witness it. May I, and my young companion, join you?"

He gestured outward, inviting them onto the porch.

The woman and child stepped onto the creaky, whitewashed porch, taking the two wooden rockers across from James.

"It's good to see a young woman who still knows Robert Johnson."

The lady gave a small smile. "I am older than I look. I had a very good teacher who showed me that music could open my mind to unlimited possibilities. He made sure I paid attention to all of it, where the music came from, why it took the form that it did, and where it might be headed.”

“Then you had the very best kind of teacher.”

“Yes, the very best,” she said. “How rude am I? We forgot to introduce ourselves. This young lady is Emily.”

“Good to meet you, sir,” Emily said, nodding slightly in his direction.

“Likewise.” James turned his head to the woman. “And your name is…?”

“Rain.”

“What an interesting name you have there,” James said.

“Emily gave it to me some time back.”

He looked back at Emily. “That is a very good name.” He paused for a breath. “You see and understand everything, don’t you, tifi?”

Emily smiled.

“It’s in the eyes. My pitit fi was the same way. She was so hungry to learn everything. Whatever new thing fell into her gaze, she would research it, dissect it, and then consume the results.”

“Do you mind if I take a look at your guitar, James?” Rain asked, politely changing the subject.

He looked up and said, “By all means.”

He handed the guitar to her by the neck. Rain brought the guitar to her and placed her fingers in position.

“Do you know who Robert Johnson was, Emily?”

“No, sir, I do not.”

Rain spoke. "His story is a legend in the world of the Blues, Emily." She slowly played Crossroads. "It was said that he was not much of a musician, but one day, he decided to change that.

"Now, in Mississippi, there is a place in the middle of nowhere where two dirt roads cross each other and continue on. It was said that it was there Robert met the Devil. He offered up his soul to be able to play well. The Devil accepted his offer, took the guitar Robert was holding, tuned it, played a few random notes, and returned it to him. From that time on, he could play like no other. Since then, anyone who has held a guitar and tried to play the blues, rock, country, or other various genres has been influenced by the sounds he brought back from those dusty roads."

"What really happened?" Emily asked, a hint of skepticism in her voice.

"I really do not know, little one. I believe he very much like you. He looked at everything around him when it came to sounds and music, absorbed it, and used it. He watched what others did and then made it his own. He was hungry to learn, and no force could stop him once he set his sights on that path."

James was speechless. The sounds coming out of his guitar were just like Robert's, as if he were playing on those old records.

At the end of the song, Rain started to return the guitar to James. He shook his head. "Could you play me something else?"

She nodded and strummed a haunting melody. James recognized it as Eric Clapton's Tears in Heaven.

Rain played the music without words. Every note was delicate and deftly done. James himself did not need the lyrics to feel the loss it represented.

Emily spoke while Rain continued to play. "Have you always lived here, sir?"

"Yes, I have, as did paran mwen yo—my parents. My Papa lived here in this spot, and my Mé lived next door at that time. After they got married and my granparan passed on, they made this land one.

"For me and my Sarah, there's no other place we want to be. Our friends and families live in these other homes. We support each other through times of happiness, sadness, heartache, and even death."

James turned and asked Rain how much she knew about the Bayou.

Rain looked up from the guitar and smiled. She stopped playing, took the guitar from her lap, and placed it gently beside her seat.

"The Bayou," she started, "is an area deep in the lands of Louisiana swamps, stories, and mythology. It is a place where new life begins and ends in the breath of a moment. It is hidden from the sight of most who come looking for it. If you become lost there, you might never be found. It has been said only God and Death can maneuver easily through the Bayou," she said, with a twinkle in her eyes. "And a man named James."

James laughed. "I've gotten lost in there plenty of times, chère. I just had enough sense not to panic and do something foolish—like puttin' my foot down where it didn't belong."

"Is it really that dangerous out there?" Emily asked. "More dangerous than almost any other place in the world—because you do not expect anything when it happens."

"But it looks beautiful out there," she said staring into the waning night's shadows.

"At times, yes," James said. "Sometimes you get onto a raft, lay back, and enjoy the ride, going with the flow of the water. You can see the sunlight cutting between the leaves, turning the water into diamonds." He paused for a moment. "It is so peaceful that if you listen long enough, you can hear and describe every bird singing. You can also hear the music made by those who lived, loved, and died here."

Rain spoke. "Do not be fooled by the quiet. There are things that cannot be heard until it is too late. The predators of the Bayou, alligators, snakes, large cats…And humans."

James's expression changed as he spoke. Emily could tell he was deep in thought.

"There are those who get so lost out there, they lose their minds. There are some who think they rule the land and that anyone trespassing true or not needs to be shot on sight. And there are still others who believe that if you don't look or act like them, you need to be gotten rid of, like you were some sort of disease."

Steady tears streamed down his face.

"God, how I miss her," he said.

"Who did you lose out there?" Emily asked.

"My daughter. She's the one I told you about."

Emily stood up, stepped over to James, leaned her head on his shoulder, and hugged him. "I'm so sorry for you."

James sniffled, shook his head as if to chase the ghosts away, bent his arm, and lightly patted the crown of Emily's head. "Thank you, ti kras. It is much appreciated, but it happened a long time ago. Memories catch up to me every so often."

"What happened to your daughter?" Emily asked.

He sighed. "If you sit back down and have some iced tea with me, I will tell you about her."

Emily returned to her chair. James picked up the pitcher, poured some tea into a glass, and handed it to Emily. He turned and silently questioned Rain, who nodded politely, accepted the drink, and then placed it beside her.

"Abigail," he started, "was truly a gift from God for me and Sarah. From the moment she was born, we loved her unconditionally. When her eyes opened for the first time, we saw that I'm excited to be here look. That look never disappeared."

He picked up his tea, took a sip, and set it back down. "She never stopped looking or learning. She wanted to read before she could talk. She wanted to run before she could crawl." He smiled. "She wanted to know how the stars and the sun moved before she even knew what they were. By God, we showed her all that we could, and she still wanted to know more."

"She sounded like a handful," Rain said, smiling. "A mother's love and a father's joy."

He smiled back at Rain. "Sometimes, a mother's hell and a father's frustration. I don't know how many rodents, lizards, insects, and other things she would bring back to the house for me or Sarah to identify. I swear to God, my wife nearly had a heart attack or passed out from fright on a weekly basis. Even I took a step back every so often from whatever she had in her hands or in her wagon.

"She wasn't afraid of any of it. I think that was our biggest mistake with her—we never taught her what fear was."

James's eyes swelled with pools of tears from a happy thought. "My daughter devoured the information all around her. When it came to music, no one could shine a light on her. I taught her to play piano, the guitar, and the drums. She taught herself how to play the flute and the violin. She could play any instrument she put her hands on.

"And when it came to singin', she sang as if she were part of the choir of angels that greeted the Children of God through the Pearly Gates of Saint Peter."

"What happened to her?" Emily asked, trying not to be rude by interrupting.

"She sacrificed herself to save our community."

"Sarah and I were teaching the children of the community at the time. Nothing in particular mind you, just some English, a bit of math, music, and other things of that nature. It was just enough that if they wanted to learn more, they could. But for the most part, the families just wanted their children to learn only the basics. Abigail also helped out by tutoring anyone who asked her, including some of the mothers and fathers themselves.

"Now, there were people who took offense at the Black community learning more than they should have. One of those groups was led by Parson John Mathers.

"John of the Marsh is what we called him around here.

"He used the Good Book to judge and to rule what others could and could not do. Instead of teaching love for one another, he used the Bible to create fear and hate throughout the land.

"One day, he stepped down from his soapbox and went out into the world, claiming God had told him that we all needed to be saved by him. He had a small flock of worshippers who followed him and sometimes even carried him on their shoulders because he taught them they were unworthy to look at him or stand on the same level as him.

"His travels inevitably brought him into our area. He first asked us to stop instructing the people of the community. We told him no.

"He became upset and made threats against the town, saying God had declared it was wrong for us to learn so much. We ignored him. He tried to get our attention by throwing rocks and shouting vile slurs, but we continued to teach.

"They decided to burn down the church where we held school. He claimed we were corrupting God's home. The man had his sheep carry him to the church, where he would set it ablaze.

"So up on their shoulders they took him, chanting Glory be unto Him. Sometimes I wondered if they meant John and not the Almighty.

"As they reached the church, we all ran out of the building, knowing he would make good on his threats. We had no police to stop him. None of us wanted to challenge the Parson and his flock. So, we lowered our heads and stepped back.

"John was placed down onto the ground, and the flock made way for him. He strode forward toward the entrance; his tattered Bible curled in his left hand and a torch lifted in his right.

As he approached the stairs, he turned to his flock and said, 'I do this for the glory of God. May He take back what was His and cast the animals that dwell here back into Hell.'

"He turned around to throw the flame and looked directly into the eyes of my daughter, Abigail."

~*~

"She had been telling me repeatedly to challenge John.

"'He cannot be ignored,' she said to me more than once. 'If you stand up against him, he will back down and leave. He is as much a coward as those who follow him. With you in front of him, others will back you up.'

"Sarah and I were afraid that if we got involved, others would be hurt. We thought that by ignoring him and staying out of his way, this would blow over that he and his bootlickers would leave sooner. "Abigail had other ideas."

~*~

"They stood face to face. The old man wore a black suit, black tie, and black hat. My daughter stood on the third step, wearing her Sunday church dress-an almost unnaturally white dress that seemed to glow.

"Not a word was spoken between them. You could just tell they were measuring each other up. He would think of something to say, then stop. He would raise the flame or the Book as if to use them, then lower them again. He moved as if he were going to push her aside then stopped.

"I have looked into John's eyes before, and I saw hate, contempt, and greed. He had the eyes of a wannabe conqueror. He wanted to take over it all and change it to suit his needs and his God. He believed that no one could stop him.

But as he looked into Abigail's eyes, he most assuredly felt fear. He might have seen something in them he had never seen before in the eyes of anyone else he had faced. Maybe it was wisdom. Maybe it was focus or determination. Or maybe he saw what she saw, all that he was, reflected back at him.

"She didn't cower or lower her eyes. She never took her eyes off his."

Emily listened to what James said about his daughter. Something flashed through her mind, and she turned toward Rain. Her jaw slackened slightly as she struggled to find the right words, whether to ask a question or make a comment on what she thought.

Rain's head was tilted slightly downward, a teacup resting near her lips. A small smile crept across her face.

"Hush, little one. Do not give up the ending before the story is complete."

Emily returned her attention to James, sipping her iced tea.

"Most of his flock did not see what transpired. They had their heads down in prayer. The ones who did walked away from him later that night.

143

"John of the Marsh curled his lips into a sneer and took a step back. He pressed the Book against his chest and tried to regroup before addressing his followers.

"'On this day, I will hold back my hand to vanquish the evil that resides here. God has spoken to me and said that He will smite this place with His own hands and that I should holster mine. We shall step back from this to let Him do His work. We shall return when God decrees it so, to help cleanse this land. Beware the wrath of the Lord.'" Then he turned back toward his people, his movements unnatural. He spun around to look at Abigail one last time, pressing the Book so hard against his chest you could almost hear a rib crack. Finishing his turn, he walked to his group, which stood up and surrounded him, chanting again, and they left our community.

"Abigail stepped up the remaining stairs of the church and quietly walked inside. As proud as I was of her, my heart felt crushed that she stood there, and I didn't. She protected our town when I should have.

"What really hurt me in that moment was that it changed her. My Sarah told me that she was still our little girl just a little more focused, a little more determined.

"But I saw something more than she did. I saw an understanding and an acceptance of what was to come in the way Abigail stood there.

"She never spoke about what transpired. Sarah and I never pushed the issue.

"Again, another mistake I made with her one that may've changed things.

"Abigail still smiled, ran around, played with others, and learned all she could. But I could see that she was only playing the part. Behind her eyes, inside her mind, something else was working.

"A few weeks later, about a couple of miles away from us, John and what was left of his parishioners were preparing for a big event. It was a prayer session that was going to end in a cross burning."

"They chose the home of a pastor and his family few parishes over. The pastor had spoken up about how John was interpretin' the Bible. He accused him of corrupting its meaning.

"John decided to make an example of him. He knew he had to reinvigorate his people. It was the first real action he had taken since he last faced Abigail. That confrontation had caused a rift in the flock some became enlightened and walked away from this false man of the cloth, while others were enraged that he hadn't pushed her aside and finished the job.

"The pastor and his wife tried to defend their home but were subdued, beaten, and tied up. They and their three children were powerless to stop what was about to come. John of the Marsh decided to burn the cross in front of them and their home.

"When the sunlight was no more, they set up the cross and prepared to light it. As he strolled to the spot, he heard murmurs and gasps coming from his followers behind him. He turned around to see their wide eyes staring past him—to his right.

"Out of the dark shadows of the marsh, wearing the white dress, was Abigail. The parishioners noticed that there wasn't even a spot of mud on her dress as she strode toward the pastor's family.

"John stood frozen in disbelief. The chants his followers had been speaking dwindled into confused silence. In their place came whispers 'angel,' 'ghost,' 'spirit.'

"She reached the children first and untied them. Then she spoke to them, and they headed in the direction from which Abigail had come. Then she untied the parents' restraints and thy followed the direction of their children followed last, making it to the tree line. The pastor said he tried to grab Abigail's arm to take her along with him.

She moved away from him, shook her head, and said with a small smile on her lips, "Do not worry about me. Everything will be fine.

Your children and your wife are waiting for you. Go now and do not look back."

She then turned around and walked toward John.

"Again, the pastor wanted to snatch her up and take her to the boat with him, but something held him back. There was a feeling that what was about to happen needed to. He felt he was only a witness to what was about to occur.

The family said that at the other side of the trees, they found a small wooden raft tied to their dock. His wife asked where the girl was, but he said he couldn't find the words to tell her what had transpired. He boarded his family on the raft, untied it, and pushed it off.

"In between the trees, the family caught glimpses of what was Abigail standing in front of John. They could hear the Parson's rants and raves, but they didn't know what he was saying. The last image the pastor saw before the water carried them away from the scene was John slapping Abigail across the face."

~*~

"In the early morning hours of the next day, I was awakened by a knock at the front door. Sarah was still fast asleep when I got up to answer it. Standing in the doorway were my brother, a few neighbors, and the pastor. I had never met him before, though others in our community had. He had been knocking on doors half the night, looking for someone who knew of a girl in a white dress who had come to their home and saved them.

"I became afraid of the answer I was about to find. I rushed to Abigail's room and called out to her, but there was no response. I pushed open the door and stood at the entrance in horror.

"She wasn't there.

"I woke Sarah and told her what was happening. We were dressed and out the door within minutes. We followed the pastor and his wife back to their home. My thoughts and dread slowed the time in my mind. I know it should've only taken less than half an hour to get there, but it felt like years."

~*~

James stopped talking and licked his lips. He took another drink of tea and looked at his two guests. He saw Emily sitting politely, listening to every word he said, and knew she was drawing a picture in her mind of everything happening in his tale.

He turned toward Rain. He tried to read her expressions, searching for anything that would reveal her emotions, but there were no signs to be found. He felt that she was either indifferent to the story or that she had heard it before. James wasn't sure why, but he felt it was the latter.

He placed his drink down and noticed that it was still cold after all this time outside—that the ice cubes had not melted. He looked around at his home and the surrounding houses. He couldn't put his finger on it. Everything looked as it should, but something was off. There was a gnawing feeling he could not describe. He felt he wasn't home anymore, even though he could see that he was.

"Where was I?" he said.

"You were heading to the house of the pastor, sir. Your daughter was not in bed, and you were told a young girl in a white dress had confronted John of the Marsh," Emily said.

"You definitely remind me of my pitit fi. I used to tell her bedtime stories, and if I didn't finish, she would bookmark the place in her mind and remind me of it when I started back up."

~*~

147

"We ran onto the land where the pastor resided, and I started to search the area for some sign of her. As we approached the lot, my wife and I began calling out her name, hoping she would respond. Sarah's voice grew more agitated each time she spoke our daughter's name. She forced herself to sound positive, but the agony of the soul has a way of revealing its true feelings.

"I fared no better when calling out her name. I kept telling myself I should have kept a closer eye on Abigail. She had been too focused on something, as if she were planning for something big.

"I had meant to confront her and talk to her about what was on her mind, but she had distracted me—intentionally changing the direction of the conversation. She had asked where the book of Aesop's tales was and if I could read it to her. She said she wanted to hear my voice telling her a story. That was the day before the incident.

"The group moved toward the house and noticed the blackened cross placed nearby. The closer we got, the overpowering smell of burnt wood, gasoline, and charred meat became.

"I heard Sarah scream and ran toward the burnt cross. Something had caught her eye. The closer she moved to it, the heavier her steps became. She ran out of breath and fell forward onto her knees.

"I caught up with her and looked down. I thought she had collapsed, but she was staring at something in her hands. It was a piece of plain white cloth, but bright. The edges were brown and ragged. Sarah clutched it to her chest, whispering, 'Please, sweet Jesus, please no.'

"When the others reached us, I stood up and continued my trek to burnt remnants of the cross. I steeled myself for what was coming next. I do not know how my legs moved, or how my heart kept pumping."

~*~

"There are no words to describe what one must feel when losing a child. What's even worse is when you grab hold of them, pull them into you, knowing full well that there will be no words, no hugs, no kisses, no heartbeat against your chest.

The child you have loved since before their birth, the one you swore you would protect and die for is no longer there for you to protect.

"In that instant, I realized I had failed my daughter."

"I stared at Abigail, who was tied to the blackened cross. A thick length of rope was wrapped around her throat and tied off at the top. Her arms were strapped to the vertical board, and her feet dangled. What was left of her skin was charred and blistered. The dress was no more than a few strands of fabric hanging loosely around my daughter's precious body.

"I removed my shirt and placed it on the ground next to me. I freed her from the burned wood, picked up my shirt, and wrapped her small body in it. I held her against my chest and just sat there on the ground, rocking her, comforting her, and praying for a miracle or hoping this was a nightmare I only needed to wake up from.

"Parts of my sanity returned just enough to realize that Sarah had sat down next to me. I wrapped my arm around her, holding on tight to my family.

"One week later, we buried her. During that week, mourners came from everywhere to say goodbye. Some had never even met her before. They came because they had heard the stories of a young girl who stood face to face with a madman, saving both a church and a family from danger.

"There were a few of John's parishioners who showed up on our doorstep to apologize and ask for forgiveness. I nearly came to blows with them, but Sarah came to their rescue, kissed them lightly on the foreheads, and forgave them. She held nothing against these people. Her anger and grief were focused on John.

"As was mine."

"After we laid her to rest, I turned all my attention to finding John. Nothing else mattered—either I would see him tried and executed by the courts, or I would do it with my own two hands. I didn't care which.

"I tracked down every lead I could, but it was to no avail. There were rumors of him running around stark naked, screaming nonsense about the dawn before disappearing back into the marshes. A few people claimed to have seen him, but then nothing. No more rumors, no more sightings, no evidence that he was still out there.

"It was like he had dropped completely off the face of the Earth.

"I personally think he got lost in the Bayou and put his foot in the wrong place."

~*~

"How long did it take for you and your wife to move on with your lives?" Emily asked.

"Honestly, we never did, and I don't think you ever can at least not one hundred percent. Throughout the course of the day, you always think about what she would have thought about this or what she would have done about that.

"All those who have passed in your life are only one thought away from being back in it. The only way to keep the ghosts of what ifs from taking over is to accept that you cannot change what has happened—and to know that those involved would want you to keep going."

Emily asked, "Did the followers who came to your home give you any idea why he did what he did to Abigail?"

"The ones I talked to said she never took her eyes off John. She seemed unconcerned that they might step forward to help him. He grew very agitated, and yet she remained steady and focused. Some heard him say they were all sacrifices, that they were nothing but steppingstones, and that they were not worthy of God's gifts. By that time, most if not all had left the area."

"They didn't try to take Abigail with them either?" Emily asked.

"I think they had the same reaction as the pastor did. It's possible this was something beyond them, something they weren't able to interfere with. It was like something pushed them away from what was about to happen. The best way I can describe it is Giants on the Playground."

"What do you mean?" asked Emily.

"It's a saying. There are moments when all things come together, presenting themselves in one place—like a playground, or a line drawn in the sand. And then, you have those whose presence is larger than life itself. To some, the words giants or gods come to mind.

"When they face off, you get this feeling that you do not belong there. Even if you stayed and watched, you wouldn't be able to comprehend what was happening."

"Did you ever find out what she said to the Parson to upset him so much?"

"I never did. Some of John's flock came to me in the later years telling me the same things the others did that they too heard parts of the conversation between the two, but they also had this overwhelming feeling that they had to leave."

He took another sip of his tea.

"I still wish I knew what she said that night to make him so angry to make him do that to her."

"I told him he was going to die alone."

James turned toward Rain, his mouth open, eyes wide with shock and amazement.

"I told him that he was going to die alone and that I felt sorry for him."

He turned again, watching as a small smile crossed Rain's lips behind her glass of iced tea. A single tear rolled down her left cheek.

"Hello, Papa."

Chapter Eleven - Abigail

James sat there, unsure of what he had just heard. The woman, Rain, had called him Papa. His daughter used to say that every so often, just to make him smile. Abigail was always so formal, so polite but every now and then, she would call him Papa to remind him that she was still his little girl.

"I don't know what you're tryin' to prove by saying that to me," James said, "but I really don't think it's funny."

Rain lowered her glass, placed it on the table, and looked deeply into James's eyes.

Damn if that wasn't the same look Abigail carried in her eyes, he thought.

"I know my outward appearance is different from what you remember, but be assured inside, I am Abigail," Rain said.

"How can that be? She's been dead for..."

"More than fifty years, Papa."

James leaned toward Rain and touched her knee. She was as solid as Emily had been when he hugged the little girl.

"Are you a ghost?"

"Not quite," she said, her face unreadable.

"Are you an angel?"

The smile returned. "Not quite," Rain said again.

"Then what are you?"

"I am the caregiver, the life taker, the protector, and the destroyer of the young. I comfort and care for the sick. I punish those who throw away their lives for selfish reasons. I protect the ones whose foundations are ripped out from underneath them. I give guidance to the lost. I welcome those who have no one to welcome them."

"That seems like a lot."

"That is no more than what you do. You have been a father, a brother, a husband, a teacher, a preacher, a musician, a protector, a caregiver. You showed me what was black and white in life. You made me understand that to live in the shadows of both is to allow others the opportunity to manipulate your decisions and actions."

Emily saw the change in Rain's features.

The knowing smile, the one that made Emily know that Rain had more answers than she let on to, faded. The sparkle in Rain's eyes darkened. The warm glow of her skin, the light that comforted others in their darkest moments, dimmed, making her now feel tired, cold, and alone.

"You made me understand and feel that I was loved. I knew I was important to you, and—" she stifled back the tears, "and you would do anything to make me feel, safe and protected."

Rain's body and mind crumbled. She cried, shaking from the weight of emotions and the choices she had made both in life and after. She slid down to the porch deck, curled her legs toward her chest, and hugged them tightly.

James had never seen his daughter cry that way, but every nerve and every sense in his body told him that the woman before him, no matter her appearance, was Abigail.

He moved from his chair and knelt beside her. He brought Rain's head to his chest, enveloping her in his arms exactly as he had on the day he found her in the pastor's field.

She released her legs, crossed her arms over her chest, and locked his arm between them. James rocked her gently, whispering that it was alright. Rain, through the tears and sobs, kept repeating how sorry she was for leaving.

Emily watched as two people who had loved each other without hesitation became father and daughter once more.

James brushed some of Rain's hair aside and lightly kissed her forehead. She calmed down, a soft smile of contentment spreading across her face.

An unspoken amount of time passed before Rain regained some of her composure. Reluctantly, she released his arm, stood up, and offered her hand to help him rise from the porch.

James returned to his seat, and Rain to hers. She tried to steady herself, bringing her emotions back under control. James remained silent, unsure whether to ask what had happened in the field or to wait until his daughter was ready to speak of it herself.

That decision was taken from them both by a curious little girl sitting on the porch.

"You told John of the Marsh he was going to die alone, and you were sorry for him." Emily carefully gathered her thoughts before asking, "What happened between you two? Why did you say you felt sorry for the man who ended up murdering you? Why was he so mad that you said that?"

Rain turned her head toward Emily, and a smile grew once again. With that, Emily felt all was good in the world once more.

Rain looked back at James. "Was I like that? Cutting straight to the chase and never forgetting what was spoken or left unfinished?"

"Worse. You would wait for an answer, tear into it, and then the questions would start all over again—until you had exhausted every possibility."

"I think I would have made a good psychiatrist."

He laughed.

She turned back to Emily and sighed before speaking. "That night at the pastor's house was his breaking point. His people were leaving him, and a small girl was haunting him everywhere, probably even in his dreams."

"What do you mean?" Emily asked.

"My father told you about the night I confronted John on the church steps, silently staring him down. That was not entirely true. I stood face to face with him and spoke one word one word that no one else heard but him."

"What did you say?"

"I said hello to him. I added to it an all-knowing smirk that drove my mother crazy with exhaustion."

She turned and looked at James. "You know the smile. The one where she tried to teach me something new and fascinating, and I would just sit there, listening quietly as she explained it to me. She would ask if I understood the material, I would smile at her, and she would storm off, muttering to herself."

"Was she mad at you?" Emily asked.

James laughed. "No no, ti kras. My Sarah realized that when Abigail gave her that smile, she had already known the lesson she was just humoring her."

"I was not humoring her," Rain corrected. "I loved to listen to my Mé. Her voice was like listening to a robin sing. The rhythm of her speech was like the waves gently crashing onto the rocky shore, over and over again."

"I thought crashing waves were loud and distracting," Emily commented.

"Not to me. When you have the opportunity, go to an ocean beach at midnight. Place your feet on the still warm white sand, lean your head back onto a small mound, and stare up into the star-filled sky and the dark spaces between them. Without seeing the waves, you will hear the steady clap of water crashing, followed by the quiet fizzle of millions of bursting air bubbles as the remnants of the wave roll back into the sea—only to be overtaken again by another wave heading toward the shore."

"That was what it was like listening to her. A slow, consistent rush of sound, carrying my mind to the possibilities of dreaming what was beyond my reach and what I needed to do to make my dreams a reality."

James could hear the crashing waves Rain had just described. He could smell the salt water in the air. A warm summer wind brushed across his face. It was faint and barely audible, but for a moment, he felt as if he were standing on the beach, yet he knew he was still on his porch, nowhere near the coastline.

Rain smiled at Emily. "We do not need to go there right now, little one."

Emily, looking as if she had drifted deep into thought, refocused her eyes and blushed. "Sorry."

With that, the sound, smell, and feel of the ocean dissipated.

"O Bondye mwen! What just happened?" James asked, looking confused and unsure of what was going on.

"I am sorry. The moment was taken over by her," Rain said. She glanced around the area before returning her focus to the porch. "Our time here grows short. I really did miss this place. So many memories," she said, speaking to no one in particular.

"What do you mean?" he asked.

Rain brushed her father's question aside. "As I said, I was haunting him. The night at the church was not the first time John of the Marsh saw me, but it was the first time we stood face to face." James looked puzzled. "How many times had he seen you before that night?"

"More than a few."

~*~

"In the days before he came into our town, I heard the parents of the schoolchildren talk about a madman. They said he wore the clothes of a preacher and walked the Bayou with a flock of followers, preaching from the Good Book. It was believed that he would be coming here to restart his sermons.

"There were those in the parish who feared what he might do while he was here. Some spoke of asking the law to step in and bar him from entering the community. More than a few people thought it might be best to ignore him, hoping he would leave quickly. In the end, most took this position and did nothing. They chose not to get involved, believing others would take care of it.

"As you know, I did not agree with that point of view. To me, they were simply afraid to step outside their circle of comfort. They focused on what was best for themselves rather than what was best for our community, our friends, and their families.

"On a warm midday afternoon, a group of white men and women walked into our town by way of the rocky dirt path we took to Baton Rouge. They were dressed in simple, oversized hooded robes gray, black, and brown. The hoods were pulled low over their heads, obscuring their faces. The sleeves hung loose and baggy, covering their hands as they walked when the arms hung low. When their arms were bent in prayer, their hands were clasped in front of their faces.

"The bottoms of their robes dragged along the ground, stirring up road dust. Amid the swirling dirt, cloth, and moving bodies, strode Parson John.

"He wore a simple black suit with a white shirt. His tie was nothing more than a black shoelace, held together by a gold cross, hovering near his upper chest.

"In his hands, he held his copy of the Bible. It looked old, and the leather cover was worn either by the weather or from being wrung in his hands. He would beat it on the podium repeatedly to make a noise, then point it toward his faithful flock.

"As I followed him and his group around for the next few days, when you thought I was searching for unknown creatures, and listened to him preach his sermons. I wanted to know what he was truly saying.

"I focused not on what he said, but on what was left unsaid. His voice emphasized certain words, each carefully chosen, leading me to his true meaning.

"He spoke of believing in change, of ensuring that everyone was on the same level in life. But what implied was that there were certain people trying to rise above their station and that they needed to be brought back down to more of an 'acceptable' level.

"He claimed that if we understood each other, it would lead to better communications for all of us. But in truth was, he wanted to understand how the town and its people worked so he could break the community apart like a fine porcelain vase. Once shattered, it could never truly be put back together as it was. There would always be flaws, cracks, and missing pieces, rendering it worthless.

"He told the people he wanted to bring everyone together for a single purpose, so they could to change and strengthen the community.

"John spoke of fighting evil, dispelling darkness, and baptizing the town in holy light and goodness, so its people could move forward with God's blessings.

"The truth behind the last part of his sermon sent shivers from my head down to my toes. When the words darkness and evil leapt from his lips, he turned his attention to one of the community's Black members. When he spoke of light and good, his eyes sought out a white member of the community. He churned up ideas of hate, greed, and envy in a town that had always been known for love, sharing, and looking out for one another.

"With what I saw and felt, I decided there might be a way to shake him up and drive him out.

"I put on my Sunday dress and shoes both white and bright and followed him throughout the communities. At every event, I kept my distance but made sure I was just outside his line of vision.

"Whenever he was about to look my way, I would slip behind trees, bushes, or the corners of houses doing whatever I could to evade his gaze.

"In the beginning, his followers never noticed me, their heads bowed in silent prayers and misbegotten praises. But I knew I was affecting him. His speeches faltered. His train of thought fractured. Instead of focusing on the people in front of him, his eyes began to wander.

"The day before the church incident, I could tell he was purposely searching for me in the crowd, trying to make sure his mind was not playing tricks on him. I had him so twisted up that I never made a public appearance. His diseased mind started to convince itself that I was always there, always watching."

When Rain paused her story and stood up from her chair, Emily seized the opportunity to ask a question. "So why did you stand in front of him on that day?"

"You can only fight from the shadows for so long. Eventually, the enemy will dismiss you as nothing more than a fleeting thought or the apparition of a forgotten memory. But when you stand before them—at the right time and place—you become more than just a ghost. In their eyes, you are now a nightmare made flesh," she said as her face, eyes, and clothes began to change.

The muscles around her cheeks and jaw tightened, revealing the sharp outline of her skull. Her warm bronze skin dulled to a morbid gray, accentuating the deep hollows of her jowls and sunken eye sockets. The irises of her forest-green eyes darkened into pools of coal-black, surrounded by an eerie glow of spectral white. Her dress of shifting colors turned filthy and tattered, its fabric peeling away into ghostly strips of spiderwebbed cloth that fluttered and twisted as if caught in a hurricane though there was no wind.

The air around her thickened, heavy with moisture and methane. The stench of unburied, decomposing bodies rotting in blood-soaked mud on a sweltering summer's day filled the space.

From her slightly parted, blue-gray lips came the haunting echoes of tortured wails screams of lost souls swallowed by time and space.

The color drained from both James and Emily's faces. What they saw before them was no longer a beloved child or daughter, no longer a trusted guide or dear friend, but the true essence of who Rain was.

Death, personified.

An expression flickered across the unearthly creature's face. It was not hatred. Nor was it hunger. It was the look of a mischievous child who had just played a trick on their parents. She wore the broadest smile, and her darkened eyes glowed with laughter.

The familiar-looking Rain stepped out from the grim version of herself, now light, bright, and positively devilish. The other image stood there for no more than a second before crumbling into a pile of dust on the porch and blowing away.

The pair facing her relaxed. James glanced around, making sure the image had truly vanished.

Emily, however, looked upset. Her expression was more angry than relieved. "Not. Funny."

Wiping away tears of laughter and steadying her breathing, Rain said, "You are quite correct. But oh, how I wish I could have done that when I confronted John. I would have frightened him out of our area, shattered what remained of his sanity, and my life would have continued."

The smile disappeared.

"Alas, it was not to be."

Rain glanced down, brushing off her dress as if clearing away dust that wasn't there. Then she turned to James, locking eyes with him.

"Now we come down to it. This is the point where everything changes and questions are answered."

~*~

"As my father said, a few weeks after the incident at the church, whispers and rumors swirled around the community that John and his people were on the move once again. They were now focused on the nearby pastor's home, a few miles to the south, deeper into the wetlands.

"So, after the sun had set, and after my parents retired to their bedroom, I slipped out of my room and went into my closet on the other side of the hallway. I put on one of my brown dresses and the boots I wore when I went into the swamps. I packed my white outfit into a carrying bag, then left the warmth and security of our home and ran into the darkness, in search of a monster.

"Now, Emily, going out into the swamp is a very dangerous thing. Even in broad daylight, you could step on something that might bite you, trip over a hidden root, and find yourself headlong in a bog. And anyone who ventures into the Bayou alone at night is either insane or suicidal.

"I do not think I was either of those things but then again, youth often trumps fear.

"I knew the land. I had walked past every rock, tuft of grass, and puddle of water an innumerable number of times. I could have navigated that place blindfolded and come out unscathed, just by listening to the sounds.

"I trudged quietly trudged through the darkness and the mud. When I heard something approaching, I adjusted my path, listened for it to pass, and then continued. I could have taken one of the dirt roads leading that direction, but they twisted and turned too much. It would have taken me the better part of an hour to get there not to mention the increased chance of someone spotting me. Three miles through the swamp would take me only thirty minutes.

"About half a mile from my destination, I spotted a raft tied to an old tree stump. You can sometimes find rafts like that around. People use them for fishing, visiting friends down the slow-moving waterways, or simply lying back on them on a lazy afternoon, watching the sky drift by.

"I untied the rope and pushed off toward my destination, steering the raft with a long-broken branch lying nearby. That, to me, was either a lucky coincidence or a sign that someone else had used it for the same reason.

"I saw flickering lights between the trees, just about a hundred feet away. The brilliant flashes of white and yellow, the towering, shifting shadows, and the crackle of wet burning wood told me I had found the place I was looking for."

"I made sure I got as close as I could to the creek's bank without crashing into the muddy side. There was a small platform extending out on the far side of the pastor's house. I knew it was there from one of my previous expeditions. I caught the edge of it and tied the rope around a post that held the pier in place. The pastor and his family always welcomed visitors who came to their home, whether by land or by water, and was happy to talk to them for a while.

"But on that night, the visitors who arrived on his land were not welcome, and they did not come to talk.

"I stepped off the raft, removed my brown clothes and boots, and put on my white clothes. I took special care not to get anything dirty as I made my way toward the pastor's front yard.

"I hid behind a large tree and snuck a look at the gathering. There were no conversations among John's followers, their attention was entirely on him and his words. Every minute or so they would all join in with 'Amen' and 'Praise thee.' John, on the other hand, was the one who was full of words.

"'The Devil has always been inside the hearts of men!' he announced to his flock. They nodded in response.

"John stood at one of the far edges of the bonfire, his shadow cast high up onto the tallest tree, looming over his followers.

"'The Evil is hidden deep inside and can escape if we do not keep a constant vigil. If it is kept in check, it does not grow.'

"A chorus of 'Amen' rippled through the flock in unison.

"'These diseased creatures,' he said, turning his hand toward the pastor and his family, 'will procreate and spawn even more of their kind. What they want to do is taint the souls of our fair and righteous people and give Satan a clear path to God's golden throne.'

"'They say we are all God's children, but that is a lie. They say they want to pray with us. What they really want is to prey on us. They speak of the Gates of St. Peter, claiming they await us all, they lie to you. If you follow these foul, black-skinned creatures, they will surely escort you straight into the Gates of Hell, where their Master awaits you.'

While he ranted and his people nodded in agreement, I chose this moment to free the family and give them a chance to escape toward the raft. No matter how brightly I was dressed, I prayed I could make it over to them unnoticed. I hoped the madman would keep the group's attention.

"Hope, I learned later, is often the last prayer for a cause that was doomed to fail more times than not.

"As I was about to cross the threshold between the trees into the open field, a quote from a book I had read entered my mind. I did not know if it was John's sermon that sparked the memory, or the way the trees created a gated entrance, but the words of Dante's Divine Comedy appeared in front of my eyes:

Through me you pass into the city of woe:

Through me you pass into eternal pain:

Through me among the people lost for aye.

Justice the founder of my fabric moved: To

rear me was the task of Power divine,

Supremest Wisdom, and primeval Love. Before

me things create were none, save things

Eternal, and eternal I endure.

Abandon all hope, ye who enter here.

"And with that, I straightened my dress, pushed my fears aside, and stepped into my very own Hell."

~*~

James interrupted Rain. "I found that book and several others in your room a few days after your death. I don't remember purchasing them, nor do I recall ever seeing them on the shelves with the other books. Where did you get them from?"

A sly, cunning smile crossed her lips and lingered. "Do you remember when John announced a book burning to remove the 'corrupted' books from the sight of man and God?"

"I remember. On the day it was supposed to happen, you could hear him screaming and scolding his people from the other side of the town square." Something clicked in his mind. "What did you do?"

Rain's grin widened. "The night before the burning, John was giving another one of his unity sermons, and all of his followers were focused on him. I slipped into his tent unnoticed, found the box of collected books, and took them."

James let out a low chuckle as realization dawned. "So that's why he was in such a rage the next morning."

"Exactly. The screams and curses you heard were him blaming everyone but himself for somehow 'misplacing' the books." She laughed softly. "I think that rattled his followers a little. They may not have walked away from him that day, but there was no doubt his hold over them was shaken."

With that, she returned to her story.

~*~

"As the pastor moved out of the clearing and toward the raft, I saw John step away from his pulpit, lock his eyes in the direction of the escape, and raise his hand in preparation to give a command. I stepped into his line of sight, forcing him to focus on me.

166

"His eyes widened when he saw me. As I said, he had seen me a handful of times before—whether in reality, in his imagination, or in his nightmares. And yet, there I stood before him again, unchanged.

"'YOU!' he hissed.

"'What are you doing?' I asked. 'You are supposed to be a man of the cloth, just as he is. You follow the Book of the Lord, and yet you tie him and his family up.'

He remained motionless, but his wide-eyed confusion narrowed into a glare of defiance. 'How dare you.'

"'What gives you the right to do that?' I pressed.

"'He does.' He glanced upward. 'God said there will be false teachers who will secretly introduce destructive heresies.'

"John took a slow step to his left, moving in a deliberate pattern, attempting to circle me and block my escape path.

"'He is not a true man of faith in the eyes of God, so the words he preaches to others is falsehood.'

"I stood my ground, unmoving, allowing him to pass behind me. My focus remained on what was left of his followers. They did not move to help him. They simply watched us, the parson, and the dark angel in pure white, waiting to see who would triumph in this verbal chess match."

"'The words you speak are from Second Peter, Parson,' I said the Passage clearly enough for the others to hear. 'But false prophets also arose among the people, just as there will also be false teachers among you, who will secretly introduce destructive heresies, even denying the Master who bought them, bringing swift destruction upon themselves. And many will follow their sensuality, and because of them, the way of the truth will be maligned in their greed, they will exploit you with false words; their judgment from long ago is not idle, and their destruction is not asleep.'

"I saw, with those words, a few hoods turned in question and concern. If John was surprised that I knew the verse word for word, he did not show it. He completed his circle around me and stepped closer.

"'Are you calling me a false prophet, you blasphemous child?'

"'You say that others who preach are false. But what if it is you who has slipped down the wrong path?'

"'God has pointed out to me what path I am to take,' he declared, raising his hands and lifting his voice so that his people could hear him. 'He came to me in a dream. A blinding bright light surrounded Him! His voice boomed in my mind. He told me to go forth and cleanse the Earth of filth and lies—to make the land pure, so that when He finally arrives, the path He walks will not soil His feet.'

"'Amen,' came the scattered chorus of voices behind me. The voices were not as strong in their commitment of belief as they sounded moments before.

"The Parson continued on. 'And then I awoke from the dream, knowing what I must do next. The sacrifices I must make to fulfill my vision of what's to come. So, tell me, Child, what do you make of what I saw?'

"'That even Satan, The Fallen One, can transform Himself back into an Angel of Light, when it suits His purposes,' I said in the simplest of voices.

"There was a flash of movement, a spark of pain on my right cheek, and then the cold slap of dirt against my left before everything went black."

~*~

"I awoke to find my arms tied in opposite directions along the horizontal board of the cross, my neck bound to the vertical beam. My face was swollen, and I tasted blood from my split lip. In my right ear, a high-pitched hum rang endlessly. The smell of gasoline was

168

everywhere. I had no sense of how much time had passed since I was struck.

"He stood there before me, a sneer on his lips and the gleam of crazed victory in his eyes. In his right hand, he held a lit, makeshift torch.

"'Where are your words now, child? What can you say to save yourself from the flame?' He waved the torch around, twirling it like a prize. He reminded me of Rumpelstiltskin, on the verge of claiming everything he had worked for.

"'As you can see, the last of my followers have left me because of your lying forked tongue placed doubts of me in their minds. You haunted my meetings and continually disrupted my plans to cleanse this land. So, what can you say or do to stay my hand from ridding this world, and me, of your mischievous and foul presence?'

"He stood face to face with me, waiting for his answer.

"A tear slipped from my left eye and rolled down my cheek. A small voice leapt from my lips and delivered itself unto his ear.

"'I am sorry.'

"His grin broadened. 'What, pray tell, dear little girl, are you sorry for, hmmm? What on Earth and in Heaven could you be so sorry for? I am enthralled about what you're going to say to me to sway my hand and my judgement.'

"'I am sorry that you will die alone and unloved. I am sorry that you will be forgotten. I am sorry that no one will miss you.'

"That superior, almighty gleam of victory darkened and disappeared in his eyes, becoming vacant of any humanity inside them. the corners of his righteous all-knowing smile crumbled. His lips thinned and lost their coloring.

"With the last specks of sanity leaving his eyes, he released the grip on the torch.

"I watched as it defied gravity for a fleeting moment before surrendering to the inevitable.

"It fell toward the ground, accelerated and then ended its journey with a thump… and a whoosh.

"I remember the flash of light. The heat of the all-consuming flame, and a soul-ripping scream that tore itself away from my throat as the darkness swallowed me whole."

~*~

"I awoke screaming. My skin felt like it was melting from my muscles. My lungs inhaled fire and exhaled tears. The rope that held me to the scorched boards slackened slightly but still kept me captive. My mind screamed between insanity and the loss of control over my life.

"A cool sensation touched the tip of my left ear. The pain consuming my entire body dulled to this one point. It lasted only a moment before the agony tried to reclaim its hold. Just as another scream reached my lips, ready to break free into the world, the nape of my neck radiated the same soothing sensation. This time, it flowed down my spine and across my shoulders. I wondered if this was a blessing, or a torture of pain and pleasure intertwined.

"The answer came from the sky above."

~*~

"A fog settled over me. As it enveloped the area, the heat from my flesh turned it into a mist that cooled my skin, stealing away my flesh's pain. My mind still echoed with the remnants of suffering, but even that began to fade to a murmur.

"I lifted my head from the noose's hanging position and cautiously opened my eyes. I could still see nothing but the lingering flash of light from when he lit the fire.

170

"I tilted my head skyward as much as I could. A layer of mist covered my face, sending a tingling relief through my skin. Two small drops slipped into my eyes. The blinding image dissipated, and at last, a blurred vision of the field came into sight.

"It looked to be early morning, just before sunrise. The landscape appeared to be a fusion of grays, browns, golds, and blacks.

"I took a deep breath to calm my nerves, bracing for the agony that would surely come from my scorched lungs. To my amazement, the mist entered my nose and mouth, soothing the pain within. I exhaled deeply, releasing a breath of unexpected relief.

"Then I looked at my bound arm and caught my breath.

"The skin on my left arm was an uneven patchwork of healing and charred flesh or perhaps the reverse was more accurate.

"The mist slowly dissipated as the morning light filtered through. As it dissolved, shifting shapes emerged within the swirling colors, like figures forming from thick brushstrokes in an oil painting. My eyes strained to make sense of the scene, to translate it into something real.

"And then, emerging from the veil of colors just above my height and a few feet away, I saw her.

"A woman's face.

"The interplay of browns and golds gave her the appearance of a bronze statue, an ancient goddess materializing from the mist, approaching me.

"Her hair was long and wavy, flowing outward from her shoulders. Her skin glowed as the morning light reflected off her, making it seem as though I was staring straight into the sun. She wore a traditional tunic draped over her shoulders, leaving her arms and neck bare.

"What stood out most were her eyes. As I said before, everything around me was gold, brown, bronze, and black—everything except for those eyes.

"They were the deepest, darkest shade of green I had ever seen. Even the most vibrant leaves in the Bayou on a warm spring day could not match the richness of that color.

"In her hands, she held two things tightly. In her right hand was a long golden sword, its blade catching the sunlight and reflecting it into my eyes. In her other hand, she had a firm grip around the back of the neck of an old, naked man.

"It was John."

~*~

"'Look at her!' the woman screamed into his right ear, pointing her sword at me. 'Look at what you did to her! You took the life of a child. A child! An innocent, and you erased her from the fabric of life.'

"'She was a violation of—' John tried to sputter out his throat was squeezed tighter around the edges.

"'She was a blessing to all who knew her—her mother, her father, her friends. Anyone who met her felt secure and happy to be with her.'

"'God told me to go to the light and turn away from the darkness to know my true destiny.'

"Through clenched teeth, the woman said, 'SHE WAS YOUR LIGHT! She was there to help you find your way back to the right path. You extinguished that light, and now all that remains for you is darkness.'

"With that, she released her grip on him, and he crumpled to all fours.

"She walked toward me, her sword at her side. Without a word, she removed the ropes from my neck and arms. I fell from the cross, but she caught me carefully, cradling me against her chest. With her touch, all the physical pain I had felt disappeared. The screams in my mind were washed away by my slowing breath.

"I don't know how long I remained in her arms. It felt as if I were asleep in my father's embrace. There was no desire to leave that moment.

"But that was taken from me by John. His voice shattered that peace. His words reawakened the thoughts of pain and fear.

"'She is an evil serpent in my garden he hissed from where he lay on the ground. She slithered around the edges and struck my flock whenever she had the opportunity. Each poisonous strike thinned out my followers until only a handful remained. She and her kind do not belong in my or God's Garden. It is my duty to remove them so It can grow stronger. She is Lilith to me, the Whore of Eden. She was the first, and if I get my chance, I will ensure that she and every other nigger who stands in my way and ruins my garden pays the same penalty.'

"I opened my eyes to see my killer standing. He looked toward the woman.

"She moved me away from her body and stood up to face John. The sword she held ignited into flames as she advanced in his direction. I saw both figures within my sight.

"'Your time is done, John,' she said. 'This is not the field where you burned her. This is not the field where you made your stand. When she died, you died. Your heart gave out. You collapsed right there. You are no more. Death is coming to take what you have left away. Death's chariot awaits to carry you to Hell. It will drag you into the Abyss and make you pay for what you did!'

"'You lie! My God will not abandon me at my time of need.' he hissed.

"The field and sky disappeared instantly into a swirling gray mass and then the same Deathly image I had shown to you was now revealed to him, in place of where the Woman had stood.

"The hollow screams from her lips pushed him backward. He fell down and curled himself into a ball, tucking his head into his knees, trying to hide from the figure standing over him.

"'Beware the coming dawn, for I will come for you. You shall be devoured by the blackness you have created in your heart and live in the void you left when you removed her from the light. Now! Begone!'

"With a final, anguished scream of "'No!' from his lips, the gray mist wrapped around him, and he vanished."

~*~

"As the gray mist slowly dissolved and the field reappeared, the woman's appearance also faded, leaving behind only the white tunic and her pale-bronzed skin. She turned and moved toward me. I should have been afraid of her after what I had witnessed, but I was more curious about what had become of John.

"'He returned to the world of the living," she said, without me asking.

"'I thought you told him he was dead?'

"'He was, for a moment. But here, a moment lasts as long as it needs to, though never forever. He has returned to his body, but his mind is now lost in the gray—never to return.'

"'Am I dead, or am I here just for the moment?'

"'Both. You have died, and your body is destroyed. There is no return for you. As for the other part of your question—we will leave this field of sorrow whenever you feel ready to move on.'

"'How can I do that? This place will always be with me. It was my first chance to do something great.' My eyes welled with tears, and my insides trembled. My mind raced with emotions and thoughts of everything I had gone through. 'This place will also be part of a nightmare that will never have an ending for me.'

"The woman knelt before me, brushed my left cheek, and wiped away the tear that had fallen. 'I understand,' she said. 'My own nightmares continues, even now, as I sit before you. If you dwell on what has happened, be it good or be it bad, you will never be able to move on from that moment. You will remain trapped in an endless cycle of what ifs and what could I have done differently.'

"She took a breath and spoke again. 'To move on, you must accept it and understand that it can no longer be changed. That is true in both life and death.'

"She ran her hand gently down my right arm, and the burnt cloth of my white dress was suddenly whole again undamaged.

"'How did you do that?' I asked.

"'I thought about it and then made it happen,' she replied.

"I took a step away from her and looked down at the rest of my dress. Seeing my sleeve restored pushed the whirlwind of emotions to the back of my mind.

"'Is that it? I mean, is that all there is to it?'

"'Yes. The mind and soul are very strong here. Some accept what they see, while others understand it can be something else.'

"I straightened my back, locked my arms at my sides, and closed my eyes. I pictured my dress exactly as it had been before the burning and told myself that was how it was supposed to be.

"I stood there for what felt like a minute before opening my eyes. What I wanted to be, was. Not a stitch was out of place. The hem my mother had sewn was exactly where it should be. The fabric gleamed bright white, with flickers of other colors flowing in and out of sight colors I had decided to add.

"I looked at the woman and smiled. I spun in place, letting the fabric swirl and ripple through the air. The trembling fears and uncertainty faded, replaced by a quiet joy.

"Then I stopped smiling. I put on a serious expression, cleared my mind except for one image, and looked directly into the woman's deep green eyes.

"I felt the change wash over me. My skin and hair returned to what they had been before. Everything was restored except for a small burn mark on the inside cuff of my left sleeve.

"A soft smile crossed her lips as she nodded in approval. 'Are you ready to leave here, Abigail?'

"I took one last look at the field as the morning light filled the sky.

"'This,' I said, waving my arm outward, 'is not real. This is a memory that I want to walk away from. So yes, I am ready to go.'

"Her left arm extended outward, fingers pointing toward the area of the trees where I had entered the field. Between the two crossed trees, a warm, inviting golden light glowed.

"'After you, Abigail. It's time for you to leave this place of Woe and Pain.'

"I took the lead and walked toward the exit. Just before stepping through, I grasped the woman's hand.

"'You know my name,' I said, 'You have said it many times, but I do not know yours.'

"She smiled. 'What name would you like to call me, Abigail?'"

"I gazed up at the blue summer sky. A few clouds drifted between the high tree line and the ever-enveloping blue. I lay quietly on a raft, which spun in slow, lazy circles and half-moons. I could feel the warm summer breeze brushing over my skin before continuing on, playing tag with the stream as it moved forward.

"In my mind and on my lips, I recited a poem my mother had told me days before my death, as we sat together beneath the large weeping willow. She leaned her back against the bark of the tree while I rested my head on the apron of her skirt, listening as she read Through the Looking-Glass, and What Alice Found There. The last poem was the one that stayed in my mind:

'A boat, beneath a sunny sky

Lingering onward dreamily

In an evening of July --

Children three that nestle near,

Eager eye and willing ear

Pleased a simple tale to hear -- Long

has paled that sunny sky:

Echoes fade and memories die:

Autumn frosts have slain July.

Still, she haunts me, phantomwise

Alice moving under skies

Never seen by waking eyes.

Children yet, the tale to hear,

Eager eye and willing ear,

Lovingly shall nestle near.

In a Wonderland they lie,

Dreaming as the days go by,

Dreaming as the summers die:'

"As if on cue, a second voice joined mine to finish the verse. Though it was not my mother's voice—the one that had always filled me with joy, it was still welcoming to my ears.

"'Ever drifting down the stream—

Lingering in the golden gleam—

Life, what is it but a dream?'

"'Hello, Aurora,' I said to her. I sat up on my raft and looked toward the bank. The old wooden makeshift raft of logs and interlaced rope twisted once more before righting itself parallel to the shore. I glanced slightly over my left shoulder, looking at her with a contented smile.

"As I had said before, she looked every bit like an angel of vengeance, and yet her green eyes were warm and friendly when she gazed at me. My raft continued downstream as she walked along an uninterrupted path she had created for herself.

"'I am sorry to disturb your peace.'

"'You could never bother me. I was just dreaming of what was.'

"Her face grew a bit more serious, if that was even possible. 'It's time,' she said.

"I nodded, perhaps not in full understanding, but I knew that something was about to happen and that I had to be present for it.

"The raft maneuvered itself toward the bank where she stood, guiding me toward a wooden dock that had not been there before.

I tied a rope between the two, and with Aurora's help, stepped onto the platform and walked toward the path.

"I moved close enough for her to hug me and kiss me lightly on the crown of my head. Her hugs always made me feel like I was in the safest, most serene place possible.

"She released me, took my hand, and we walked down the small dirt path. The trees we passed by changed from the ones I remember from my home on the Bayou to very grand, ancient-looking trees with which I was not overly familiar.

"Further down, a group of children ran around those trees, jumping over small bushes, lying flat on the hillsides, and some were playing a game of Tag.

"A thin, dark-haired boy seemed to be It. He was older than most of the others. I could see that he could easily overtake any one of the players whenever he pleased, but he did not.

"He always just seemed to miss touching them on their shoulders. When it came to even the smallest of children, he would trip or slip on something, and they would escape, their laughs, giggles, and joyful screams filling the field of play.

"Then, as if someone had flicked a switch, he halted and moved toward Aurora. He looked deep into her eyes and said, 'Yes?' The word seemed less like a question about her presence and more like a question about something unspoken.

"Aurora gave a series of nods in acknowledgment. He reacted by throwing his arms around her.

"When they broke the embrace, I could see tears in their eyes and a mixture of sadness and joy on their faces.

"Aurora said, 'This is Yosef. He will be walking with us.' Then she turned to him. 'Yosef, this is Abigail.'

"And for him, that was enough.

"He came up to me, gave me a small hug, and said, 'It's a pleasure to meet you.'

"The other children came over, taking turns hugging both Aurora and Yosef before returning to their area of play. They stood there as if they were waiting for something to happen.

"At the end, a small red-headed girl no more than four years old came up to Yosef. He lifted her up, jiggled her lovingly in his arms, and whispered in her ear. Her eyes lit up from the message, and she grinned.

"He put her back down. She took two steps away, turned around to look at the crowd of kids, and announced, 'I'm it!' before running full speed at them. The others broke away in screams and laughter. The game was back on.

"Aurora, Yosef, and I continued our travels down the dirt path. No words were spoken between any of us. Aurora and Yosef held hands, nudged each other, and leaned against each other's shoulders, but their eyes remained fixed on the path ahead.

"Once we were out of sight of the children, the path changed from dirt to cobblestones of different widths and lengths. There were symbols etched on top of the larger ones. I did not recognize them at the time. I thought of asking Aurora what they meant, but I decided it was not the moment to question her.

"The stones and the path they created became larger until the path itself turned into a small road. The road led into an open clearing with no trees, save one. The road then spiraled around until it reached the base of the lone tree.

"The sky above was still the deep blue of the afternoon, outlining the towering tree we approached. It had a massive base, deep roots, and a vast canopy of branches. The leaf-filled branches spread so low they nearly touched the ground. Scattered throughout were various sizes of yellow fruit. The large shadow of the tree cast itself over the open field.

"Deep in the shadows, barely visible, stood the silhouette of a man near the base of the tree.

"Aurora spoke. 'That is Etz haDaat Tov V'ra, or the Tree of Knowledge of Good and Evil. It is one of two trees that changed the direction of Man's destiny. The other is called Etz haChayim, or the Tree of Life. The children of your beliefs know of that one.'

"I nodded.

"'Over time, and with the changes in beliefs, those two trees became one.'

"She turned to Yosef, kissed him lightly on his cheek, and said, 'Why don't you continue on? I will follow behind you in a few, okay?'

"'Okay.' He removed his hand from hers. 'L'hitraot, Katia.' Then he turned to me, nodded, and said, 'Kol Tuv, Abigail.'

He then walked into the tree's shadow.

"'He told you to be well,' she explained without me asking.

"'What did he say to you?' I asked.

"'He said I will see you soon, Katia.'

"'Did he give you a name, too?'

"'No. He has always known my real name.'

"She looked at me, and I returned a quizzical look.

"'He is my brother.'

"My understanding of the situation solidified in my thoughts.

"'So that would mean the man under the tree is your father?'

"'That's right. He has come to collect us.'

"'How long have you been separated from each other?'

"'For some time now. My brother and I arrived here at about the same time. He was overworked and starved to death in one of the concentration camps outside of Warsaw. I died in one of the furnaces, as did many others that day and on other days just like it. Our father was sent to another camp near Austria and worked in a smelting plant. He survived the experience.'

"'And your mother?'

"'Just before everything happened, she was in America visiting her sister. For obvious reasons, she stayed there until the war was over. She returned to look for us and our father, but she couldn't find us or him. She went back to America and decided to live there, where at least she had loved ones living near her, since we had been lost to her.

"'My father was so grief-stricken by the loss of Yosef and me, and by the knowledge that he couldn't save us, he went into self-imposed isolation as a penalty to himself. He didn't want to face my mother as a failure who couldn't protect his family.' She took a deep breath in before continuing.

"'That is one of the reasons you are important to me, and why I came for you. You and I went into the fire and came out the other side. We both had a strong belief in our faiths and our families. I didn't want to see you get lost in your nightmare. What was unknown to me was that you were going to be the one who would take over this position, which I will now vacate.

"'Was I the only choice?'

"'No. There were others who gave me a name and might have taken over, but their families came for them before mine.'

"'So,' I said, 'what will happen next?'

"'There are things you must know and understand before I depart, things that I and the Others like me have laid out for you and those that will come after you.'

"Once I understood what needed to be done and what was to be expected of me, she hugged me, turned around, and walked down the path of stones.

"Just before she entered the tree's shadow, she shuttered off the guise of Aurora and became Katia.

"To describe the image of the young woman I saw walking toward her father's open arms, I would say that she looked a little like her brother and a picture that I once saw of Anne Frank on the book of her diary.

"A moment later, they went around the base of the tree, and they were gone."

~*~

"What were the symbols on the stones?" Emily asked.

"They started out as the Hebrew alphabet, or Ktav Ashuri, were imprinted on the first stones we walked on. By the end of the path, the entire Hebrew Bible, the Torah, was etched onto the stones."

"Every word of it?" James asked, realizing the story of Aurora was over.

"Yes. Religion and family were a big part of her upbringing. Her father, also named Yosef, was a Rabbi before the invasion of Poland. So, the history of her people was etched into her mind, just as the letters and words were etched onto the stones we walked on."

"How did you figure that out about the symbols on the stones?" James asked.

"Her mind, her thoughts, and her experiences are pressed into who I am. Everyone who takes up this mantle leaves a part of who they were and what they did. So, Aurora is a part of what I became, and what I became will be passed on to the next." Rain looked at Emily and said, "That is who you will become."

James' eyes widened as he fully grasped what was being said.

"So, if she is here to take your place, then that means…"

"It is time for you to take me home," she said, her eyes full of tears. "Look around, Papa. As familiar as this place is, somehow it does not seem quite right, does it?"

James gazed beyond the edge of his porch. The tree was larger than he remembered. The colors of the neighboring houses were off. The break between the field and the Bayou didn't look as dark.

"Where are we then? I noticed everything around me looks the same, but there is something more going on here, isn't there?"

"This," Rain spoke, "is the Place of Making. It is where you enter before you go to the next Realm. It is a bridge between Life and Death. It has been known by many names, including Gehenna, Barzakh, Naraka, and Purgatory. It is the next step beyond the previous life and the one to come.

"It bends to the mind, heart, and spirit. You shape it from your thoughts, whether positive or negative. When I died, my fear, pain, and horror of my death overlaid the area. I would have been lost there without Aurora. She focused me past the hurt, which allowed me to change and leave the place I had created.

"When Emily first arrived, her world for most of her life was in her room. For her, that room was both a horror—fearing she may never leave, and a comfort, knowing her loved ones came to visit her. Her dreams were also in that room. She had music, art, books, and a small view of the outside, giving her hope that someday she might be able to spend more time out there. It was her escape she could not achieve. She created her own bubble of life and chose to leave it when the right moment arrived."

"With a little help from you," Emily added.

Rain nodded and smiled at her little companion.

"Pitit fi?"

"Yes, Papa?"

"Let the illusion go."

"Yes, Papa," she said with a nod.

~*~

The outer tree line, the old porch they stood on, and the houses of the quiet community blurred and melted downward into the ground. The tree in the center of town still stood tall. The yellow fruit it bore appeared from the depths of the leaves.

The large cobblestones Rain had described spread outward from the tree and into parts unseen by the eyes.

Emily looked down at her feet. On each stone, a name was etched into its hard, sandstone-colored exterior.

"Each stone represents a child who stayed here while I watched over the land," Rain said. "It did not matter if I collected the child or if they came here on their own—a stone was etched for them."

"In over fifty years," James said, looking over the rocky field, "the numbers would be in the…"

"Millions. Yes, I am aware. War, starvation, indifference, disease, greed, and so on."

Emily looked at the stone beneath her feet and read the name. It was her name. She knew there were other girls who had come here with the name Emily, but she knew this one stone had been made for her.

"Emily," Rain said, bending down to her knees to face the little girl eye to eye, "what am I to do with you?"

In response, Emily wrapped her arms around Rain's neck and held on tight.

"Not what I expected for an answer, but it is one I will gladly accept," Rain said, returning Emily's gesture in kind.

The two held each other close for a time. Emily leaned against Rain's chest, and Rain's chin rested lightly on the top of Emily's head.

"So," Rain said, "what am I going to do with you?"

"You're going to kiss me on the forehead and tell me everything is going to be alright."

Rain kissed her and looked down to gaze into Emily's eyes. "You will be alright."

"Not everything is going to be alright?"

"If everything were alright, there would be no need for you, me, and the ones who came before us to do what we do. We are here because nothing is perfect, and we are doing what we can to make it a little better. If everything were alright, then no child would pass before their parents. If everything were right, there would be no greed, hate, jealousy, addictions, or sickness.

"I do know you will be alright. You have what is required to do this. A good and caring soul that is full of youthful optimism and tempered understanding. You will be able to handle what will come and you will be able to help whoever needs it in a world that is not alright. You will be the hope for those who are lost."

Rain let out a sigh. Emily felt as if she were about to release something she had held onto for a long time.

Emily saw Rain's eyes flicker back and forth from green to brown and back again.

"Abigail," Emily said.

"Yes?" Her now brown eyes were full of tears.

"It's time for you to go. Your father is waiting for you."

"Okay."

Emily placed her lips on Abigail's forehead, hugged her, released her, and stepped back.

Abigail stood up, leaving the image of Rain where she knelt. She wore her white dress and shoes. Her hair was pulled back and placed in a bun at the back of her head. She turned and nearly ran into her father's welcoming arms. He hugged her tightly and carried her into the shadow of the tree.

Emily listened to them talked while they disappeared around the base of the tree.

"Abigail?"

"Yes, Papa?"

"When will we see your mother again?"

"Don't worry. She will be here in a moment."

When the last sight of Abigail and her father was no more, the image of Rain crumbled to dust at the feet of Emily's silver shoes.

EPILOGUE

"I think he's finally waking up." Conner heard a man say from somewhere in the painfully bright room. A large hand rested on his right shoulder.

"Don't move too much, Conner. There's an IV in your arm, and we don't want you to accidentally pull it out."

"Whrggg..." was all Conner could manage.

"Better not say too much yet. You were dehydrated when they found you and barely breathing. There was a tube down your throat to help you for a while. We removed it not long ago." His voice seemed to move in another direction, away.

"Go get his parents, nurse. Tell them the good news."

"Yes, doctor," another male's voice replied, followed by the soft hiss of a sliding door opening and a faint click as it closed.

"You gave your parents and us quite a scare a couple of times, young man. We're glad you're back with us."

A finger and thumb pressed against his left eye, forcing his eyelid open.

"Now, this is going to be a little bright."

A painful flash of light made him jerk.

"I'm sorry. Your eyes will readjust in a little bit. You were in that dark closet for such a long time."

The sliding door opened.

"Oh my God, Conner!" A voice that he knew to be his mother. He hadn't heard in forever it seemed to him.

Her arms wrapped around him, squeezing him tight. He felt wetness on his cheek where hers pressed against his.

Another set of arms grabbed him by his right shoulder, and his father's voice bellowed into his ear, "You're okay now. We got you, and we're never letting you go again."

Conner started to cry because, after everything had happened, he finally realized that he was safe.

"I'm going to step out of the room for a few minutes to give you some time together," the doctor said. "When he's ready, I believe the police will want to ask him some questions."

The door slid open and shut again.

The three in the room, a family reunited, held on to each other in silence.

~*~

Conner's vision cleared over the next few minutes, he began to take in the images around the room—the television mounted to the upper right, a whiteboard, and pegboard on the wall toward the foot of the bed, and a digital clock on the right, opposite of the sliding door.

"Wherrrrr?" he strained to say again.

His mother answered first. "You're in the hospital. The police found you three days ago, and an ambulance brought you here. You were so pale, so thin that they thought you were..." She trailed off, unable to finish the sentence.

Conner tried again; his throat was still raw. "No...where...?"

His father spoke next. "You were taken and locked in a closet a few miles from here, close to three weeks ago. The police found you by chance. The building only had a few tenants living, along with some people who may have been squatting. Someone called 911 about a foul smell coming from out of one of the empty rooms a few days after hearing loud bangs. No one there wanted to get involved until the stench was overwhelming.

"When the police arrived, they found two dead men. They may have been the ones who kidnapped you. It looked like they killed each other. The police searched the place and found you behind a padlocked door."

A wave of exhaustion passed over Conner. He fought against it, forcing himself to speak.

"Where is the girl," he took a breath, "who opened the door?"

His parents, Annie and Taylor, shared a shocked glance of disbelief.

"What are you talking about? What girl?" Annie asked Conner.

"The girl… with the gold dress..." He paused, catching his breath again. "She opened the door… the room became bright… her dress shined… her hair… like bright fall leaves…"

"No." Taylor slightly shaking his head. "No one mentioned a girl being there and you were locked in that closet. They said the lock was too high for most people to reach."

"Did she say anything to you when she opened the door?" Annie asked softly.

"She told me not to give up… that you were coming for me… that you loved me very much… that it was almost time for me to leave the room… then the door closed again… and then a bright light flashed… and then… and then, I was here."

His mother's hands trembled as she squeezed his. "Do you remember anything else about her?"

"Her eyes…" Conner whispered.

"They were the most beautiful green I've ever seen

www.ingramcontent.com/pod-product-compliance
Lightning Source LLC
Chambersburg PA
CBHW060416310726
48976CB00003B/1070